LEVEL UP

11 Steps To Building The Powerful Life YOU Deserve

Jamison Smythe

10-10-10
Publishing

Level Up
11 Steps to Build the Powerful Life YOU Deserve
Jamison Smythe
www.LevelUpSteps.com

Published by:
10-10-10 Publishing
Markham, Ontario

CONTENTS

I dedicate this book to my amazing parents,
Wendy and Dave Smythe,
for always being here for me, loving me, supporting me,
guiding me, and teaching me to live a life of gratitude and happiness.
I love you.

And of course, I dedicate this book to Solveig.
She taught me compassion and selflessness,
and I will always cherish that.

Jamison Smythe

DISCLAIMER

Before you begin, I'd like to remind you that this book is 100% my own personal opinions and beliefs on all topics discussed. There are mentions of financial and medical suggestions, as well as mindset shifts and ways to change your life to become successful. While I do believe in all of the ideas shared in this book, I cannot guarantee that your life will be totally altered or changed.

All of these thoughts, opinions, or criticisms are my own. I cannot speak for you and your situation, so please do your own research to come to your own conclusion and form your own opinion on the things in this book.

Regardless, I wrote this book to share how I got to where I am today. I am happy, positive, and enjoying life, all by altering these 11 areas of my life. These suggestions and insights have helped me personally, and I wanted to share my journey.

FOREWORD

In this extraordinary book, *Level Up: 11 Steps to Building the Powerful Life YOU Deserve*, you will learn and have the ability to rework the most basic areas of your life to your benefit! Jamison Smythe has done an amazing yet simple job decoding and explaining some of the most necessary areas to create your most desired life. With such a massive topic as life itself, Jamison is able to teach you the seemingly intimidating sections of life and make them coherent and easy to follow.

You may be confused about where you are in life; who you are and what your purpose is. You may believe that it is impossible to be happy or fulfilled in the usual happenings of your day-to-day life. Maybe you find that problems happen to you, and just seem to get worse! Perhaps you feel your relationships are not where they could or should be. Maybe it's your finances, your health, or even yourself—whatever it may be in your life, this book is for you!

Jamison has been to many of my workshops, including my Communication and Speaker Workshop, 10-10-10™, Mulberry Hill Gang, and Postulates Club. Every time I see him, I am intrigued with his profound interest and love for personal development and positive thinking. His knowingness of his own happiness is clearly defined in his thoughts and actions, and I believe that anyone—*you*—can learn this too.

This book is the starting place for your best life—a life where you will say WOW at every corner. With the principles inside of *Level Up,* you will determine the areas of your life that you can improve on and move towards to create the best version of yourself possible. Jamison has artfully proven that his practices work for him, and I am confident that they will work for you too. I highly recommend Level Up to you because I believe, as Jamison passionately states: *You deserve your best life!*

Raymond Aaron
New York Times Best selling Author

ACKNOWLEDGMENTS

First and foremost, I sincerely thank my **mum** and my **dad** for their endless support and love. They have always been there for me and have always encouraged me in what I do. They make me laugh every day, and even if their jokes are terrible, I still love them deeply. They've taught me so much over these last 18 years, and I am truly indebted to both of them for bringing me up the way they have. They are my biggest role models in my life, and I am grateful for them every single day. We laugh and we bond, and they always know how to cheer me up when I am stuck. Thank you for everything; I love you.

Scott, my older brother, has always been here to back me up and help, even though he denies it. While we do have our usual brotherly arguments, we get on well all other times. He is a kind person, and he helps me when I need it, and I enjoy our time hanging out when we do; we always have a good laugh. I appreciate every time we bond over music or a game, and I love when we work on projects together.

I am utterly grateful for **Namira** and **Taliya**, who have been with me for over a decade and where every moment with them has been a blessing. While they are not my family by blood, I nonetheless consider them the closest family I have. The love and light they share with the world is powerful and moving, and I admire their endless strength. It's been an amazing journey to watch them change and grow into their true unabashed selves—I look forward to watching their dreams come true as we move through life together. I love you guys so much.

Thanks to **Linda** and **Eric Chan,** and their sons, **Marcus, Nolan, and Ryan,** for being an open and loving family. They have been there for me during this last year of self-discovery, and I appreciate everything they have done. They are always welcoming and loving, and they offer their home for my family to stay when we are in Toronto. We often have amazing conversations about the things we are learning on this path together, and I am grateful for each and every one of them. They welcomed me into their family quickly, and I appreciate their generosity.

I am grateful for the wisdom of my publisher, **Raymond Aaron**. Not only has he been a big help in the process of getting my book completed and printed, but he is also a great teacher. I have been to a couple of his courses, specifically his Speaker & Communication Workshop, and Get Your Book Done Book Camp. I have learned much about myself and how to live a better life, the benefits of writing and being an author, and the spiritual teachings he has explained.

I'd like to thank **James MacNeil** for his passionate and meaningful insights. I met him at Raymond Aaron's Communication course, where the things he said and quoted blew my mind, and I appreciate his caring and positive attitude! He was open to my ideas when I talked to him, and I am grateful for his intrigue.

I'd like to acknowledge **Meridith Hankenson Alexander** for being an amazing human being. Although I have not met her personally, I have heard so much about her and her story. Her book, *The Sky Is the Limit,* is a very beautiful and powerful story, and it touched my heart. I deeply appreciate the love she has for her daughter, **Schuyler,** and the love she shares with the world!

Thanks to **Kat Nieh** for inspiring me. Her dedication to her travels across the globe has been phenomenal to watch, and her blogs detailing those travels are super well-written. Kat is a very caring person and I enjoy her positive vibes; she's my family! I'm excited to see where she adventures next!

I'd like to thank **Stephen Nickerson** for helping me understand the importance of passive income and living a life of adventure. He taught me some amazing things about his spiritual journeys and the things he learned. I appreciate his fun-loving attitude and passion for life!

I'd like to acknowledge my school friends, **Naomi Duhume, Jeremy Chartrand, Zaynab Elmi, Dahlia Belfer, Hannah Pittman,** and **Harmony Brown**. They have been supportive in all of my endeavors of work and thinking. Both new and old alike, I appreciate them all for being caring, fun-loving, and attentive, and for showing endless interest in me and my book's progress and completion. They light up the room when they walk in, and they are people I enjoy spending my time with. I appreciate all of them for listening to me blab on about self-development and my book, and I enjoy our time together—thank you for making high school interesting!

There are many teachers at my high school, and there are a few that stick out for me. I'd like to thank **Ms. Verreault**, the principal, for being a great head of the school; she represents it well, and she always seems to be smiling when I see her. A huge thanks to **Ms. Cain** for pushing me to achieve greatness in the visual art world, and for supporting me in my work. I enjoy my chats with her, and I appreciate all of the time I've spent in her classes, understanding more on the art and medium I work with. **Ms. Saunders**, the librarian, is always in a good mood when I speak to her, and I appreciate her generosity of allowing me to use a separate library room to work on this book. As well, **Mr. Goliath** always has a smile on his face when I walk into class, and I appreciate his positive vibes: "Make cool stuff." It's hard to beat **Ms. Mroz's** kind and caring attitude, and I am appreciative of her having to read all of my weird written works in her English and Writer's Craft courses! I'd like to thank **Ms. Harris**, who had supported me throughout my Grade 11 year and was always pleasing to talk to. And of course, I'd also like to thank **Ms. Paulin** for being such an amazing drama teacher and model. Thank you all for making a mark in my high school years!

Thank you to **Katie Jones, Sara Collins**, and all of the volunteers at **Ottawa Stray Cat Rescue**. I am grateful there is a loving organization to take in strays in my area, and I am glad they are making a difference in the world. Each volunteer has love in their hearts and is passionate to help. I am very grateful to be a part of it.

I am grateful for all of the help **Sebastien** has provided me over the last few years. He helped me get to where I am now, and I am very grateful for that, I appreciate his good mood and welcoming attitude whenever I see him!

I am grateful for the amazing photography of **Suliman Sallehi.** The cover of this book features one of my favorite photos that is within his collection, and it portrays the adventure and brightness that I feel this book is centered around.

There are many influencers, entrepreneurs, and personal development gurus that I truly admire and respect. I am sincerely grateful for the information and life-changing material presented by **Gary Vaynerchuk, Bob Proctor, Mary Morrissey, Les Brown, Tony Robbins, Earl Nightingale, Mel Robbins,** and **Tom Bilyeu.** They have all changed my view on life, and I appreciate each and every one of them!

The **Royal Canadian Air Cadets** was a large part of my life for several years. I had entered as a nervous and socially introverted kid, and came out feeling the best about myself than I had my whole life. By being involved in the program, I learned discipline and time management, and I gained so much confidence by working my way up the ranks. I sincerely thank the organization for the opportunities it had given me.

I'm grateful for the impact that **The Duke of Edinburgh's International Award** has had on my life, to help me grow outside of my comfort zone and allow me to experience things I never thought I could do before. I appreciate the connections I have made through it, the memories gathered, and the experiences I lived while doing it.

I'd like to thank **Jesse** and **Kong** at **JumpCut.** They have taught me a lot about passive income and creating financial freedom through their webinar series. They create really moving work, and I look forward to seeing where their insights take me.

Some YouTube channels that I appreciate include **Be Inspired**, for providing me with motivational videos to fuel my work. I'm grateful for **Kenneth Soares,** at **PowerThoughts Meditation Club**, for creating some really beautiful "I AM" affirmation videos, which I enjoy listening to in the morning. I also enjoy listening to the beautiful ambient sounds provided by **The Guild of Ambience,** and the soothing in-game music of **Skyrim.**

I love music. While writing this book, I listened to many different kinds of artists and bands to help me concentrate. I am grateful for the music made by the bands **Glass Animals, Arctic Monkeys, SIAMÉS, Pink Floyd, Imagine Dragons**, and so many more. Their music gives me inspiration and fills me with joy every time I listen.

I'd like to thank my cats, specifically **Piper** and **Nutmeg**, for "helping" me write this book. They always want cuddles while I am working, and they pester me for kisses. They provide company and endless love. Sometimes they like to distract me by eating my plants and running around like crazy, to which I tell them to stop, and they always seem to find their way to my lap again. Reader, I apologize if there are any typos in this book—blame these two!

CHAPTER ONE

SELF-MASTERY

YOUR BIGGEST INVESTMENT

Well, you've bought the book. You are holding it in your hands, and you are feeling...*excited?* Nervous? Afraid for what it might do to you? *Convert you!?* Well, that's great! All of those feelings are signs that you are here for a reason! Whether it be that you found this book on Amazon, have been given it by a friend, or simply bought one from me in person, you have it for a reason. The Universe has gifted you this book as it knows what you will be able to do with this information—and that is why I wrote this book!

One quick thing before you officially start: I want to say thank you. ***Thank you!***

Thank you for choosing this book as a starting point in your path of self-development. I know it is not easy to begin. It can be intimidating, ungraspable, and feel far out of your comfort zone. And let me tell you, all of those are true! In fact, you may feel that you are not ready to use this information right away, but that is okay. As one of my favorite quotes goes:

ooo

"When the student is ready, the teacher will appear." - Buddha

ooo

This is a great quote to start this book with, as it teaches so much. When you are ready for the information, it will appear. When you need this information in your life, it will come back to you at the right time, so don't push it on yourself. Though, while I don't suggest postponing your own growth, it is a different journey for each individual. Everyone has a story of how they got to where they are.

When I first started, I was very begrudged by the idea of self-help when my parents brought it up the first time. I was a mopey teenager in his early stages of high school. I didn't like people or social functions, I didn't like working, and I *definitely* didn't like the idea of making it all better. I *enjoyed* wallowing in my own self-pity! Weird, right? Well, my dad had become involved in Mary Morrissey's program, *Dreambuilder*. It was here that he learned the importance of following his dreams and expanding his mind. He had also got into the Rich Dad Poor Dad program—created by Robert Kiyosaki—which opened his eyes to the world of money and money management. From here, my dad introduced these concepts to my mum, my brother, and of course, me.

The rest of us were unimpressed with the whole idea of this self-improvement stuff. The only places I had heard about this stuff was on notebooks, pens, and too-sweet scented candles with inspirational quotes and sayings on them. My mum was annoyed with my dad through the whole process at the beginning, because he was busy buying more courses at every event. Even with this outside input, my dad stood his ground. He understood the importance of them.

Over the span of these last few years, both of my parents have become fanatics for self-improvement and are always looking for more things to do and go to. They have taught me and my brother well, and we are far onto the path of self-improvement too. Only two years later, and by the flip of a switch, I am much happier, positive, and productive than I have ever been!

So yes, it does take time. It takes a *long* time: time to understand, time to acknowledge what you are doing, and time to know what you need to do from here. No, I'm not saying you need to bust out $10K for courses right away (yes, that can happen) and read everything you can right now, but I don't suggest tucking this information away for two years and following the same path as I did. Trust me, within the time between hearing about self-improvement for the first time, to now as I am writing this, I was in a horrible state of mind: negative, self-loathing, and hating myself. I wholeheartedly don't want you to feel this way; so while I can present you with this information, it is up to YOU to decide what you do with this!

This first chapter is all about *self-mastery*. What this chapter will bring to you is the basic fundamentals of YOU. I will teach you about *yourself:* how you speak about yourself, how you treat yourself with words, and how others view you as a person—among just a few. This chapter will be packed with *very* important information to grow your *self*. Throughout the entire book, you will discover the eleven steps—or areas—that will impact your life greatly when understood and mastered. This is important stuff, so please don't dismiss it. This is YOUR life!

So, what *is* your biggest investment? I'm sure it's obvious to you now, but the answer is you! YOU are the biggest investment you can make in your life. You are the biggest thing you can grow in your life. By constantly learning, you are putting the time into creating the best version of you.

So once again, thank you for choosing this book. I know that by being here, you have made the decision to finally take action on changing your life for the better. It may take some time to understand, and it probably will, but awareness is the first step to change. I am excited to hear where you take this in your new life!

POWER OF "I AM"

To start this off, what are some of the things you say about yourself? On a day-to-day basis, people say so much about themselves that they don't even realize, and about 95 percent of the time, it's negative! How come? What exactly *is* "I AM"?

I AM is a statement piece. In fact, it is a statement piece made by YOU. The term, I AM, is a prefix for many statements used every day.

It is a self-centered thought and saying toward yourself as a person. You won't notice it, but you, your friends, and others around you will say an I AM statement regularly. An average person will say an I AM statement multiple times daily, possibly more than 10! This may not seem like much, but it is; it all just comes down to the content of the statement.

For example, if you say something negative about yourself, it leaves a subconscious imprint of that in your mind. It sticks around and, over a period of time, it will become your reality. As I said previously, 95 percent (I would even hazard at 98 percent) of the time, an I AM statement is something *negative* about yourself. With this in mind, what are some things you may say about yourself that you don't even know about?

Common negative I AM sayings you may hear and/or say yourself:

- I am stupid/dumb.
- I am a loser.
- I am ugly.
- I am a failure.
- I'm not able to do that/I can't.
- I am not someone people want to be around.
- I am uninteresting.
- I am not worthy.

These are things you DON'T want to say about yourself. If these are the types of things you tell yourself, how do you expect to live a happy life? You will go about your life always saying you aren't good enough; that you're dumb, that you are a boring person, that no one wants to be your friend, that you aren't worthy of good things. Sounds awful, right? Well, believe it or not, this is the reality for many. It may even be *your* reality!

Why are so many I AMs negative, though? You were probably told in your childhood that bragging is a bad thing. It was, and still is considered to be, seen as narcissistic and self-centered. Therefore, you most likely developed the habit of putting yourself down and not praising yourself when you did (or still do) something awesome. If you were told in your childhood that you were stupid, ugly, fat, or anything else from the list above, then you most likely have some deep down self-worth issues. Because people told you that you *were* those things—and it doesn't matter if it was your parents, friends, teachers, or even strangers—whoever it came from had made a lasting imprint on you to this day. From here, you took on the habit of repeating those same I AMs. Why? Because that is all you are used to hearing about yourself.

This acknowledgment is the start of change for your thoughts. If you are constantly telling yourself "I'm an idiot," even as a joke, it leaves a blueprint of that on your mind. *Especially* if it is used as a joke. Jokes are usually truth masked by comedy. Therefore, it can still leave a damaged mark on your psyche. You may say, "I'm stupid," when doing something insignificant, which you may say doesn't count. But let me tell you: each and every I AM you say adds up, so don't let small circumstances get the better of you.

So if not negative, then what CAN you say? Well, a positive I AM of course! Positive I AMs, just like negative ones, magnify in your mind. It's a vice-versa scenario with I AMs: negatives lead to negatives; positives lead to positives. So, if you think and say positive I AMs, you will feel much better about yourself, and it will completely change your mental attitude and mindset! These positive I AMs are called *affirmations*, which I will discuss more in Chapter 7: Mindset. There, I will go more in-depth into the life-changing habit of positive self-talk.

SELF-LOVE

Self-love is an area of life that is preached everywhere, but I rarely see it ever practiced. How come? It seems to be everywhere: on book covers, talk shows, on billboards, and in advertisements and music, and more, yet it's rare to find it being put to use. Here I will discuss the meaning behind self-love: what it is, why it's important, practicing it for yourself and others, and how it can attribute to a healthy and happy life.

So, what is self-love? Self-love is, surprisingly, exactly what it implies: the love for oneself. You may hear people talk about it a lot, but do they ever seem to actually know how to love *themselves*? I personally see many people spreading the idea and value of self-love to others, but never seem to actually love themselves in return. Do you happen to be this type of person? Whether that is a yes or a no, you must learn to practice self-love, both toward others AND yourself!

Self-love is so important. It is one of the many very important areas of your life, as it revolves around YOU. It's all about how you feel about, care for, and love yourself. What's the alternative to self-love? Simple: self-loathing and self-hatred. If you had to choose between self-love and self-hatred, which would you choose? Probably self-love, right? Most likely! Well, guess what? You CAN choose that; you CAN love yourself! It's that simple. Decide what you want, and TAKE IT. This is a powerful mindset to have, especially when it comes to what you want from yourself, such as self-love. Find out more information on this mind state later, in Chapter 7: Mindset.

Later in this book, in Chapter 4: Relationships, I discuss how self-love can be implemented around interpersonal relationships; not only how you can gain self-love from others, but how you can begin to guide others to love themselves in turn. It is quite an important section on relationships, so please make sure to take time to read it carefully.

In the end, self-love is something that should be at the forefront of your mind; your life should revolve around it. You should always love yourself—that is the whole deal behind self-love in the first place: love yourself unconditionally! Now, if you have made a really bad mistake, then, of course, you will probably not feel like loving yourself at that moment. I understand that, and you should too. But at the end of the day, it should still be bubbling under the surface of your being. So be gentle on yourself; you're human!

By having and showing self-love for yourself, you aren't being self-involved or narcissistic; you are just loving yourself for who you are! It is society that says, if you have an ounce of self-love, you are self-centered. That is the furthest from the truth! When you love yourself, you allow yourself to have the life you want, the things you desire, the things that make you happy. Without self-love, what kind of life do you live?

ooo

"To love oneself is the beginning of a lifelong romance." - Oscar Wilde

ooo

CONFIDENCE

Confidence is an attractive characteristic of successful people. You will always know who the confident person is in the room, as they portray certain characteristics. These characteristics, mentioned below, can help you become confident in yourself and in the things you do in life. Having confidence helps you with your self-worth and self-image by feeling confident in your own skin. Confidence allows you to love yourself, build a strong character, impact the lives of others, feel better in your body, and live a happier life. Confidence comes in many forms. Below are 9 examples of characteristics that will make you a more confident, lively, and happy person when put to use.

Characteristics of a Confident Person

Appearance

Appearance is the first thing you notice when meeting someone for the first time. Believe it or not, you make a judgment about someone within the first 7 seconds of seeing and/or talking to them. This means you only have a 7-second window to make a good first impression.

Communication is classified into three groups: the three V's, which are Visual, Vocal, and Verbal. Each of these V's add up to 100 percent of your physical characteristics. If you don't know these, then pay close attention; if you do, then here is a recap.

Visual communication is the first V and makes up 55 percent of all communication. This pertains to what you wear, how you stand, and how you look. One of the first things people notice about you is what you wear. Are you dressed smartly? Sloppy? Casual? Decide what kind of impression you want to make with your dress, in the circumstance you're dressing for. After your outfit, comes your posture. You will stand up straight, with your shoulders back and head raised high. I hate to break it to you, but *no one* is going to think you're a badass if your head is looking at a stain on the floor—so look up! It also improves overall posture and confidence, as it shows you are comfortable in your skin. Your face and head are the next things people notice about you. Is your hair neat? Face clean? What emotion are you displaying on your face? Confident people rarely show anger or disdain, if ever. A confident person has a smile on their face and a spring in their step. So dress well, stand straight, and smile more!

The second V is Vocal communication. This makes up 38% of your communication. Vocal communication is your voice quality: the clarity, volume, tone, and pitch of your voice. If you are a confident person, you will speak clearly, with distinct syllables, and no mumbling. You will speak at a good volume, using your diaphragm and not your throat. By using your diaphragm, you can project your voice further and with more force, with less effort than when speaking from your throat. One more thing: Never use a sarcastic tone unless the situation is appropriate. I use sarcasm a lot as part of my humor, but I still choose appropriate times to do it. Speak up, speak clearly, and speak like you own it!

The third and final V is Verbal communication. This makes up the last 7% of communication. Verbal is what you actually say: the words you say and type of speech you use. If you want to be confident, use proper sentence structure and good grammar (especially when writing), and don't use slang. If you want to be a confident person, you need to be confident in what you're saying. Have a good sense of humor but nothing too dark. Of course, it all comes down to circumstance: If you're at a formal function versus with some close friends, you will be using different types of communication, so just be mindful of where you use them.

In the Now

A confident person doesn't put important things off until a later time. They work *in the now*. They don't say, "I'll do it tomorrow," for it to never happen. They know that if there is something they need to do, they will do it as soon as they can. They manage their time efficiently, and use it to do the things that are absolutely necessary at that time. Are you this person? If yes, congratulations! If not, begin by choosing the top three things to do today, and DO THEM. Don't tiptoe around your responsibilities!

Risk Taker

Every confident and successful person has taken and continues to take risks; risks that are calculated in business and money, and risks of adventure in every other aspect of life. Many people assume that successful people (especially entrepreneurs) take risks without planning, but that is untrue. People are only successful *because* they have put the time into their work and have dedicated a long time to planning and executing their ideas. Without risks, there is no change, and without change, you cannot grow. Risks push you out of your comfort zone and allow you to grow beyond your idealized potential. Take risks in life by doing things that scare you: Go on a lengthy vacation, go on a zip line, climb a mountain, swim with sharks, or even go to a public function that you may not have wanted to do before. Do the things that scare you. Take risks and enjoy the process of change.

Take Ownership

Confident people don't make excuses. They take responsibility for their actions, own up to their faults, and don't blame others for their mistakes. They understand that *they* are the only ones that control their lives; therefore, it is their own fault if something goes wrong or is not complete. For you to become confident, start by resisting the urge to lie or make an excuse the next time it arises. Know that you are in total control of your life. If you are late, own up to it. Don't make an excuse about the traffic. SHOW UP and OWN UP.

Hard Facts

Confident people like hard facts. They don't want anything sugar-coated; just the raw data. By fluffing out the facts, an idea can get manipulated and contorted from its origin. If you get a straight-to-the-point, no-bullshit fact, it is easier to discern and understand rather than something sugar-coated and unrecognizable. So, learn to give straight answers, ask straight questions, and get straight responses back. It makes life so much easier without all the bull in between.

Decisive

Being decisive—meaning you make quick decisions—is a good quality of any confident person. By making snap decisions, you get straight to the point and save time while doing so. A good practice to get into is to start answering yes/no questions with JUST yes or no. You don't need to explain or give reasoning for things, just make the decision and roll. Another thing to practice is if you go out to eat, find what you want, decide, and close the menu. If you've already chosen, then there's no reason to continue flipping through! DECIDE and ROLL.

Judgement Free

A confident person never judges others. Never *stir the pot* or gossip about others in a negative way. You don't know their back story, their past, or current situation. Always see people as a clean slate, with no assumptions placed upon them. Confident people don't need to hurt or judge others, as they are confident enough in themselves to not look down on others.

Self-Assured

A confident person is self-assured. If you are confident, you don't care what others think about you. You are confident in yourself, and you display that confidence to the world. Caring what others think of you is one of the worst things you can do for yourself. You can't change it, so why focus on it? As well, don't compare yourself to others. A confident person is so self-assured in themselves that they don't feel the need to compare their life to another *better* life of someone else.

Be confident, and display that confidence! You are worthy of it.

Color Outside the Lines

Finally, one big attribute of confident people is that they tend to color outside the lines. This means they find new ways of doing things and do not follow the *herd* of people. You need to begin finding solutions to your problems, in new ways that you may not have thought of before. Be innovative! Do new things, execute your ideas, and see where they take you!

These were just a few examples of things confident people do and idealize. Become accustomed to doing these things, and you will soon become confident in yourself and the things you do. It takes time to learn the habit of confidence, but I promise you it is well worth the constant work! Revise these 9 characteristics of confident people anytime you need a reminder or want to track your own progress. Go out, have fun, and build your confidence!

HABITS

Habits control your life. They are everywhere, from what you do to what you don't do in your life. It has been found that more than 40 percent of your day is comprised of habits! All of that time is spent on autopilot, without you even knowing about it! Crazy, right?

Habits are actions that, over time, become ingrained in your life. If you do something every day for more than a month, it becomes routine. Constant repetition of an action or a group of actions leads to memory. The human mind is just like a memory foam mattress: One instance of sleeping won't change it, but sleeping on it for more than a month will leave a solid memory imprint. This is a great analogy to explain how your habits are imprinted on your *memory foam*.

o o o

"We are what we repeatedly do." - Aristotle

o o o

Take the example of driving to work, for instance. Every day, you drive to work (if you don't drive, then just roll with the idea). You probably take the same route to work, leave at the same time, grab the same coffee, and be at work at the same time. This is all done without you really thinking about it. Why? Because it's a learned habit. If you continually do that every day for more than a few weeks, it will become a habit.

Darren Hardy, the author of *The Compound Effect,* discusses how habits are learned over time. He mentions that a habit can be formed in only 21 days, which is also backed up by many credible sources and is a well-known fact. Just 21 days! Imagine what a difference you can make in your life if you started making good habits *today!*

There are such things as *good habits* and *bad habits.* Good habits aid you in maintaining and growing a good life. This includes health, wealth, mind, and soul. These habits help you to stay alive, be healthy, be mentally and emotionally strong, etc. Some examples of good habits are exercising, eating healthy foods, keeping your house or room clean, and saving money for necessities, among just a few. These are just a few of the habits that can make you feel better about yourself and what you do. On the other hand, bad habits are habits that are detrimental to your life and can drastically impact you in a negative way. Some bad habits include eating unhealthy foods, spending money often and/or on unnecessary things, smoking or drinking, watching too much television, etc.

If you want to live a happy, prosperous, and successful life, you need to adopt good habits, and kick bad habits to the curb. Successful people take on good habits. Unsuccessful people take on bad habits. Here are some examples of good habits versus bad habits:

Successful people...

- Eat healthy foods, drink water, and exercise frequently
- Hang around positive people who inspire and motivate them
- Read and/or listen to audiobooks about healthy living, self-help, spirituality, money, etc.

- Practice gratitude for what they have
- Set goals to achieve

Unsuccessful people...

- Eat unhealthy foods, drink sugary and unhealthy drinks, and rarely (if ever) exercise
- Hang around negative people who gossip and talk badly about themselves and/or others
- Watch TV every day
- Complain about life and what they don't have
- Don't have goals or ambitions

Now, I'm not saying you *can't* do any of the things on the Unsuccessful People chart; I just don't recommend doing them. Of course, it is okay to do these things rarely (like eating unhealthy foods or watching TV), but doing it every day is definitely going to create a long-lasting habit, and will immensely alter your chances of gaining a head-start on your new life. So, be wise about what you do!

My final thought about habits is this:

○○○

If you want to change who you *are*, you need to change what you *do*.

○○○

If you want to become the person you want yourself to be, you need to begin by changing the person you are today. To do this, you need to change the habits that have gotten you to where you are now. This means that by changing your current habits, you will get a completely different outcome. A successful person hasn't gotten successful by luck. It is the culmination of changed positive habits completed consistently over a period of time. Your *current situation* has been determined by *past habits*. Change these habits, and you get a *new* situation.

Using the power of habit for good is an incredible way of altering your life for the better. With harnessing the potential of habit, you can make changes you never thought were attainable! The situation you are in right now—whether physical or mental health, finance, relationships, hobbies, or any other aspect of life—is the result of past habits.

The next time you have the option to do or not do something, decide what the best choice is. Does it *help* you or *hinder* you? Once you do something (or don't) there is a very good chance it is the beginning of a new habit. Do not overlook what habits can do for you; they will become the leaders of your life, not you!

Decide who you want to be, change your actions to become congruent with your desired life, and kick ass while doing it. It's all up to you!

ooo

"Your beliefs become your thoughts.
Your thoughts become your words. Your words become your actions.
Your actions become your habits. Your habits become your values.
Your values become your destiny."
- Mahatma Gandhi

ooo

BRANDING

Most people associate *branding*, or a *brand*, with a company or business, which is true! But there is a very common, very misinformed version of *brand*. It's so misinformed and hidden that no one is ever taught about it in school or post-secondary, and *definitely* not in the workplace. So, what is it? Well, here is the secret brand that has been hidden from you your whole life...YOU are the brand!

You may be wondering how this is possible if you are not associated with a company brand; but whether or not you own a business, *you* are associated with a brand. Yes, you are! And the brand is YOU! YOU are your own fully-standing, fully-fleshed, thinking and walking brand! So while you may not have a *business brand*, you *do* have a *personal brand.*

Most people associate *brand* with a company or business. There is a BIG difference between a personal brand and a business brand. A business brand is the marketing presented by a company that represents and identifies them. Think of the Nike *swoosh* and "Just Do It," or the McDonald's "M" and "I'm Loving It." They are both business brands.

A personal brand, however, is very different. A personal brand is simply the way you present yourself to others and, in turn, how others remember you. This could be in the form of what you say, what you wear, what you do or do not do, how you interact with others, how you see yourself in a public light, and how others definitively see you.

○○○
"People may hear your words, but they feel your attitude."
- John C. Maxwell
○○○

Social media, nowadays, has allowed anyone to showcase their brand to the world. This can either be a great thing or a very destructive thing. It has had the ability to heighten an already devastating mass of bad personal brands in today's society. Take someone who has posted pictures of themselves drinking or doing drugs, naked, or associated with a negative group or person. These pictures, I'm sure you have heard many times, will be on the internet forever. By posting things of this nature, not only will you lose the credibility you might usually have, but you will also have a harder time finding a job that *will take you.* By far, the most important thing that can come from this is the impact on your personal brand. If you still want to post these things, then feel free; I'm not your dad. I just want the best for you and your future personal brand. So please, for the love of God, don't compromise your brand by doing stupid shit. Use your head, and make sure what you post will bring your brand up, not down!

I'm sure, now that you understand what brands are, you can pick out a few people you know who have distinctive brands. Common

15

personal brands include the Jokester, the Rebel, the Mom or Dad of the group, the Hotshot, the Player, the Nerd, the Nice One, the Fancy One, etc. These display a general synopsis of the brand associated with a person you may know. The guy that is known as the Jokester likes to crack bad jokes, play pranks on friends, laughs and makes others laugh, and is always having a good time. The Fancy One is the person in the group that dresses nicely, talks smoothly, has a good vocabulary, etc. Nothing is wrong with any of these groups; they are just some common ideas for personal brands.

A person doesn't have to fit into one of these classic groups. You may know someone (maybe even yourself!) who has a distinctive brand. For me, in early high school, I was known for being a quiet guy who always, without a doubt, wore either a plaid shirt OR the same blue hoodie every damn day. My friends could easily point me out in a crowd, or ask someone if they had "seen the guy in the blue hoodie/plaid shirt," whether they had seen me that day or not. That was my brand at that point, and I was defined by it. I'm proud to say that now, just a couple of years later, I am more of an extrovert than ever, and I'm positively influencing others and polishing my own (better) personal brand!

Now you can see how each person—business owner or not; famous or not—has a brand associated with them. So here's the big question for you:

○○○
How do you want to be perceived by others?
○○○

Think about how you want to come across to others. Decide what you like and don't like in regard to the person you want to be known as. Here are some questions you could ask yourself:

- How do I want others to describe my personality and attitude (kind, fun-loving, motivational, dominant, no-bullshit, etc.)?
- What kind of wardrobe do I want to be associated with (casual,

streetwear, conservative, etc.)?

- How do you want to make others feel (loved, strong, motivated, etc.)?
- And any other questions that can impact how others see you!

All of these questions play into your personal brand. Choose what and who you want to present as. Soon you will find you'll be known as the person who does this, wears that, makes people feel this way, etc. Remember: you don't have to be chained to one kind of brand, so feel free to adjust. Play around and have fun with it!

At the end of the day, you shouldn't care what people think of you. Do what makes you happy, and don't worry about others' criticisms—they don't matter. If your brand makes you feel good about yourself, then who cares what others think and feel about you? You should, however, think about your brand, and decide what you want to portray outwards.

ooo

In the next chapter, I'll explain the importance of time: time you have lived, and time you have left to live. I'll go over *living in the now*, and why you must do the things you want to do, when you want to do them. Don't miss this chapter, as I'll also touch on spending time wisely, planning and journaling your time, and using time to efficiently get to your goals!

CHAPTER TWO

TIME

LIFE IS SHORT

You only have so much time in your life to do the things you want to do. The average lifespan in North America, in 2018, was 80–84 years old. That may seem like a long time, but when it comes to things you want to do in life—to go to, to see, to listen to, to taste, to feel—why do so many people have regrets when they are older? Was it because they didn't have enough time to do the things they wanted to? Was it that they were unhappy? Was it because they were getting old and decided that they couldn't do the things they wanted anymore? Are you afraid of having regrets when you're older? Consider this: Why? Why have regrets?

○○○
"Ticking away the moments that make up a dull day, you fritter and waste the hours in an offhand way.
Kicking around on a piece of ground in your home town, waiting for someone or something to show you the way."
– Time, by Pink Floyd
○○○

People go through their lives caring about the wrong things. They care what others think, what the news has to say, what health problems they will get next—so many things! People are dying too young nowadays. Humans have the capability to live far longer than ever thought possible, especially now due to the type of world we live in. But why are so many not?

People die too young because of stress and lack of life satisfaction, among many other things. Most things, though, come from the dissatisfaction of life. What are you unhappy about? Your job? Your health? Your finances? Your mood? See, everything comes back to you. YOU are the only one who can change your life, for better or worse.

People have regrets due to the fact they never had the life they wanted. If only they knew that it was up to THEM, and them ONLY; would they have had the chance to be happy and love life? Now I'm talking to you, my dear reader. What regrets do *you* have?

The reason you have regrets is that you were (or still are) too scared to do the things you wanted at the time. So with the time you have left, do the things that make you happy. At the end of the day, it's hard to say how long you *do* have. Whether you're twenty, forty, or eighty, sick, healthy, broke, or wealthy, you could die tomorrow. I know it's morbid, but it's the truth!

Think of things that you'd like to do, see, get, and go to! Don't live your life worrying about future regrets. LIVE IN THE NOW. Ditch that negative "friend," go on that vacation, get that tattoo, date that person that you're scared to ask out, and if you're in school, take the courses that *you* want to take, not the ones your parents want you to take!

For example, many people don't get tattoos because they think they are going to regret them when they're older, and that they won't be able to get a "good job" with them, and that people will think badly of them, among other reasons. I say f*** it. Want a tattoo? Get one! (Of course, think about it for a bit; I also don't endorse getting face/hands tattoos right away, but to each their own, I guess.) For me, I want a *lot* of tattoos. I got my first one on my 18th birthday, and another not even a week later. So what if I regret them when I'm older? Each one will represent an important milestone in my life. I'll remember who I was with when getting it, and I'll remember the meaning for the tattoo at that time. It meant something important to me at that moment of my life, so why should I care what others think? Tattoos are awesome! Do what you want: it's your body, your experience, your LIFE.

Being spontaneous is a great way to live. It adds excitement to days that may usually be boring for you. Decide quickly if you want to do something, and do it! If you hear birds singing outside, go for a walk; if you're inspired to travel, book a trip; if you're filled with curiosity, go on a crazy adventure; or even build a snowman if the weather calls for it! If you think too much and too in depth of your current plans, you won't have as much fun compared to if you live in the *now*.

It's your life and your life only. YOU are the only captain of your life, and you are in full control of the wheel. Don't expect someone to come and save you, because it won't happen—they're trying to help themselves anyway! Screw the naysayers; they don't matter. Go out and DO the things you want to do! Enjoy your life! This is *your life* now; don't waste it. Have fun, play in the moment, and don't live a life of regrets!

TIME MANAGEMENT

Time management is so important. Using your time efficiently is one of the best ways to increase your workflow and to get things done in a good timeframe. Time management is something we all have been told to practice, but many people are *really bad* at it. It doesn't matter how they learned it; it never seems to stick. Are you this person? If so, let me teach you about time management and how it is used to create the most efficient and successful life you can have.

Time management is—*get ready for it*—the management of time! It is how you divide your time into certain areas. There are things that, as I have stated before, will help you or hinder you. Imagine if time were money. If you had $100, you might spend it a bit casually. I mean, it's only a hundred bucks, right? But if you had $100,000, you would keep it safe and spend it well, right? No matter how much you have, when it's gone, it's gone. Be sure to make every penny—every moment—count. What would you spend your "money" on if you knew you'd never get it back?

Everyone has 24 hours in a day. Whether you are the Queen, a plumber, an Olympic gold medalist, an IT tech, a stay-at-home parent, or even Jeff Bezos (founder and CEO of Amazon), you have 24 hours in every day. If you use these hours efficiently and effectively, you have an unbelievable advantage over those who do not. You will be surprised by what you can achieve by using time wisely.

Have you ever wondered how successful people have been able to create the life they want? They seem like an overnight success, don't they? To you, yes, but they have put hours upon hours, days upon days, weeks upon weeks, and even *years* into their work, to get to where they are. Successful people have used their time efficiently, and utilize it to the max. They have worked their asses off to be where they are, and they seem like overnight successes, as their results are the only things people see, not the work that was put into it!

These people have managed their time so effectively that it has become 90% of what they focus on. They don't spend time watching TV, socializing with negative and unproductive people, complaining about things they can't change, or spending time on anything that isn't constructive. Everything they do is something that helps them get to their goal. They don't want to waste their time doing things that are unimportant to their goal.

So, what do you have to do with this? Well, what do you want to achieve? Once you figure something out, decide what you need to stop doing. Ask yourself: "What do I need to quit doing that is stopping me from getting to my goal?" Write down what it is that you need to stop doing. Write down that you need to stop watching TV, movies or videos, stop talking to negative people, stop complaining, stop this, stop that. I also suggest writing down next to each one *why* you need to stop doing it.

Successful people create, not complain. Once you have written these down, now you can ask yourself: "What can I do now that will bring me closer to my goal?" Now that you have cleared out your hindrances, think about what you can *start* doing that will bring you another step closer. No matter what small changes you make, each change is another step toward your goal.

○○○
"Start before you are ready. Don't prepare, begin!"
- Mel Robbins
○○○

So, now that you have learned that time management is a big part of becoming the person you want to become, and of doing the things you want to do, what will you do with it now? Will you let it sit on the shelf and collect dust, and go back to being a person who "doesn't have time?" You DO have time, but you have to MAKE the time. Stop spending it watching another episode of *Friends!* Or, will you become the person who takes steps to cut these non-beneficial habits from your life, and DO something with your time? *What do you want from life?*

Remember to use your time well. YOU are the only one who has control over how it's spent. After all, time is the most valuable resource you have, so don't waste it. Make every moment count.

PLANNING

Planning for the future is an important aspect of time management and how it coincides with your life. I will discuss planning for goals, later, in *Chapter 8: Goals*. This section is about the importance of planning time usage for your everyday life.

I'm sure that at some point, you have had to plan for something. Whether it be a presentation, a party, a trip, you have put the time into creating the most efficient use of time for your plan. Here's a question for you: How often have you planned your *day?* Just a normal day, nothing new or important. You probably rarely, if at all! You most likely do the same things every day because you have a routine. Remember the last chapter? Habits control 95% of what you do every day.

"Most people spend more time planning a one-week vacation than they spend planning their life."
- Michael Hyatt

○○○

See, most people plan for things that are important to them, but not for their lives. I'm not saying a life-changing vacation is not important, but there are more important things to consider in life than which place to eat at on Trip Day 3. Today, and every day, is important. You need to begin to plan your days to maximize your efficiency. Imagine if you had an extra four or more hours every day to do what you want? Well, if you plan your days in advance, that is a possibility!

So, how can you maximize your time? To start simple, plan your days. It can be before bed or when you wake up. Make a list of important things you need to do today, then some things you'd like to do today. Once you get the important things out of the way, you'll be surprised how much time you have to actually do things you want to do! Right now, take out a notepad (your phone is fine) and write down the date and NEED TO DO and WANT TO DO at the top. I am sure you learned the difference between *needs* and *wants* in elementary school, but a *need* is something that is necessary to have or do, and a *want* is something that is not necessary but would be nice to have or do.

Under each column, write down things that *need* to be done that day, and things you'd *like* to do that day. These could include paying bills, doing the laundry, making lunch, going for a walk, reading a good book, etc. Decide what you need/want to do today. Next to each item, write a time frame for each one (5 min., 10 min., 1 hr., etc.); this will give you a sense of how long it should take you. When done this, write a #1 next to the most important thing, and continue writing #*n* for each thing on your list, starting with your *needs*. Get to work on them, and soon you'll see how much time you have left to do your *wants!* It's as simple as that.

Once you have a habit of this, you can push even further with planning. Another great thing to do is to plan your months and upcoming year. This sets you up for your long-term planning and lays it out straight for what you want. Make sure you read Chapter 8: Goals, as I will explain this important step to your own *overnight success*, in more detail.

JOURNALING

Journaling is a great practice to get into when it comes to time. Journaling allows you to write down the progress of areas in your life. It lets you observe where you have been, recollect your past easier, and helps you determine where you will be in the future. Let's get into it!

With journaling, you can track your progress—progress in money, fitness, relationships, spiritual journey, other important life steps, etc. Journaling is great for tracking money and where you are spending your money. This includes how much you have, where you have earned it, where you spend it, and how this helps you or hinders you, depending on what your money was spent on.

Journaling helps you track progress in fitness too. This is very important if you are taking steps to get rid of fat, gain muscle, practice for a marathon, or any other fitness goals you may have. Writing down what you did that day or week for your fitness, is a great way to see where you used to be, and to compare it to where you are now. It can be very inspirational to see these changes!

Tracking relationships and how they are changing over time is another great thing to do. By writing down someone's name and what kind of relationship they have to you, you can see over time how the relationship has changed. This is great for seeing what works and doesn't work, how they fit into your life, and if they are a good or bad person to be around.

Finally, tracking your spiritual journey can be really interesting! This could be tracking your meditation, dreams, spiritual books you have read, and more. Writing down how much you have changed during your spiritual journey is great to look back on, to recollect forgotten material, and see where and how your thoughts and practices have changed. (All of these areas will be re-mentioned within this book. Keep an eye out for main concepts on money, health, relationships, and spirituality, within other chapters!)

To track these things, I would 100% recommend getting a journal to write in; it could be from your local book store or craft store. I find there are some great ones at my local dollar store too, so have a look in one near you! Get a large, good quality journal with lined pages. This will become your daily journal: you will write everything that happened to you that day, so make sure to include the date. Write down things that happened to you, how you felt, the progress you have made in certain areas, people you talked to and about what, or anything else you want to add! Get one large enough that you will be able to contain a full year's worth of writing.

I know it sounds like a lot of work, but if you do it every day, it makes it so much easier. It can be annoying if you forget to do it for a week and try to recollect what happened—trust me, I have done this multiple times, and it is a giant pain in the ass, so keep on top of it as often as possible! Once you have a habit of writing in your daily journal, start getting smaller journals for more specific areas. Here, you can include more details and track things closer than in your daily journal.

Having these journals will really help you understand where you have come from, where you are, and where you will be. If you see you haven't changed anything for a couple of weeks or months, be ready for the same things to occur. If you journal and notice where you are, you can begin to change what has caused the same results. Enjoy your time journaling. It allows you to soak in what has happened during the day, see changes in results, and what you need to change for the future. Have fun with it!

ooo

In the next chapter, we talk money. I'll teach you about the myths you have been taught about money, the truth about money, a system to organize your money, and ways to make money on the side. Do you run your money, or does your money run you? We'll answer that in the next chapter.

CHAPTER THREE

MONEY

WHAT DO YOU KNOW ABOUT MONEY?

Many people assume money is something that is hard to attain. Most people think that it's only for those who earn the best scholarships, attend the fanciest universities, and earn the highest income from the best jobs on the planet. This is not true.

○○○

*"We buy things we don't need, with money we don't have,
to impress people we don't like."*
- Fight Club

○○○

You are in your current mindset about money, and you need to change it. Once you do, you need to take the actions to get you to where you want to be in the world of wealth.

To start off, you need to begin to think differently about money. The ideas that many people have about money are ridiculous. You were told at a young age that money is hard to make—that you can only make good money at a good job, that money is the most important thing in life, and the common "Money doesn't grow on trees" and "I'm not made of money" excuses.

The problem is that you were most likely raised on these notions and have not delved any deeper into thinking about it. You've never looked into creating the bank account you desire because you feel it is impossible. You may wonder why money is hard to make and why it always seems so unattainable. The thing is, it isn't!

The fact is that anyone, including *you*, can earn thousands upon thousands of dollars every *month*. You just need to be aware of what is available to you to do this. Once you can acknowledge the myths you believe, you can begin to change how you see money, and begin to live the life of wealth you have always dreamed about.

MYTHS OF MONEY

Money Is Hard to Come By

The majority of people believe money is hard to come by because that is what they were taught growing up. Your parents probably told you that you need to work hard and work long for good money. Without a degree or diploma, you'll never be able to make anything good. This is also enforced in schools.

The truth is, money is actually pretty easy to make. Yes, jobs are created so you can get a head-start on your income journey, but most people stay in this crevice their whole lives. They work a boring 9–5 job that they don't like, 40 hours a week, every week, for 40 years, to earn an average-at-best income, retire, and then die with very-little-to-no money, with very little life experiences, because they were tied to their job.

Money is actually a simple yet powerful resource and tool in life. As long as you can see an opportunity to earn passive income, and to take the action required, you will be highly rewarded in turn with the numbers you would like to see in your bank account.

You Can't Make Money from Home

While 95 percent of people work away from home at their job, a small number of insightful individuals make an earnest income from their front porch and couch. The majority of people (you may be included) think that this is not a "real way of making money," as it doesn't involve the physical elements of "normal jobs."

In fact, the people who work from home are totally logical in their work! More often than not, they are putting more than 40 hours into their work every week. They work overtime and weekends, and work when others are out partying and socializing. These are the people who become successful entrepreneurs because they are putting in more effort into their passions than those who work for someone else. Because 95 percent of people are trading their time for money (which, remember, is a valuable resource), they can only grow their income by-hour; but from home, you can earn far beyond an hourly rate!

These people are more insightful, and they realize their time is more valuable spent working for themselves than for someone else; they are their own boss, and they set their own work schedule. They can take as many breaks as they want, and can do whatever they want, as long as they are making money from the time they put into their work.

So, the next time you think that someone who works from home isn't doing a real job, rethink what you know now, and see the things they are doing that work for them. In the end, if you don't like these people who *make it work from home*, you need to understand that working from home is and will be the future of the economy. Find a way to get out of your 9–5 work life, and research how you can become your own boss too. Start dabbling in your interests, in your spare time, to see how you can start your own business and create other sources of income from your home. As long as you have a computer and an internet connection, you're good to go!

Investing Is Risky

Most people agree that investing money is a good thing to do, but are very wary of it because they think it's "risky." The thing is, yes, investing can be risky; that's the whole thing about it. Investing money is putting your money to use to bring back more than what you put in over a period of time. This is called ROI (return on investment), or how much you get back in return for your original investment price.

People who are actively investing actually do quite a lot of research beforehand. They wouldn't just throw their money at something or someone, and say, "I don't know what you can do with it, but give me money." No, they research extensively about what and why they should invest in a product, business, property, person, stock, or any other types of investment opportunities.

Most people see investing as risky because they don't understand how ROI works; they think it's too much work (which it is!), or that the opportunity is fake or "too good to be true."

I find it funny that many people are fine to spend thousands upon thousands to pay for formal education where they can get a degree, because they think that's the only way they can make good money. The truth is, investments may potentially cost the same amount to get started, but you will actually receive the same amount and more back in ROI! If you are still confused with what I mean, I suggest you take some time to do some research into ROI and investment opportunities that could help you.

Money Is Everything

Most people live their lives thinking that having the fattest wallet is what it's all about, and that they'll finally be happy. Well, sorry to tell you, but that's not true.

Having money is important, and we have already established that. But while money is a very important *aspect* of your life, it isn't and *shouldn't* be your life's end goal. Life is supposed to be an exciting journey, not focused upon how much money is in the bank and how much you're in debt.

Money is a tool. It should be treated as a tool and nothing else. Money is not supposed to be fretted over but used to make life easier and more enjoyable. When you use money as a tool to make more money, you have found the secret to lifetime passive income. When money is used in proper ways, such as investing, and growing yourself as a person and helping others, you become a successful and wealthy person. Don't get hung up on how much you have and how much you owe. Money makes life fun and full of experiences; it's a tool and must be used that way to create the life you want. Use it well, and allow it to work *for* you, not against you!

JAR SYSTEM

Many people don't know how to handle their money. They spend it wrong and wonder why they never have enough. Well, there is a great money managing system out there, called the Jar System. The Jar System was created by the self-development organization, Success Resources of America (or SRA for short), under T. Harv Eker. This system, by what I know and follow, is the most spiritual and valuable way of looking at and organizing your income.

In this system, there are six *jars*, each one pertaining to a specific area of your life that needs money; this includes anything and everything that you will need to spend on in your lifetime. The total 100% of your money is divided between these six jars, each jar with a specific percentage attached to it. The reasoning behind these divided jars is to divide your income in the most efficient way, so you can earn more for important things and spend less on unnecessary things.

Here, I'll explain all six jars, the percentage they make up of your income, what they should be spent and used on, and how it will affect your life in a positive way, both for your wealth and your future.

Necessities (55%)

The Necessity Jar is the largest portion, at 55% of your income, divided between your Jar System. This jar is used to pay for all of your necessities in life, such as your home bills, like heating, water, and mortgage; the food you eat; the clothes you wear; the gas for your vehicle; the technology you use; the furniture you have; and more. It's all of the things you have in your home, and need, to live your normal life. It's the things that you would usually buy on a day-to-day basis without thinking of it, such as a coffee from Starbucks, or how you commute to work.

Keep in mind that necessities will differ from person to person. For example, someone who works in IT will require more advanced technology than someone who is a sculptor. Someone who earns $30,000 a year will have to settle for a cheaper car or mortgage/rental than someone who earns $100,000. Living expenses change due to the circumstances you may be in; therefore, your necessities may not be the same as those around you.

Financial Freedom Account (10%)

Your Financial Freedom Account (or FFA) is a jar that you will put 10% of your income into, but will rarely spend. This jar contains the money that you should ONLY spend on things with a high ROI (return on investment, already mentioned) or that will make you money. This is the jar in which you need to save up money for or to put toward investments.

This is one of the most important jars (though they all are very important) because it is the "Golden Goose," as my dad has explained to me before. This is the jar that will pay for your future.

The FFA is solely for the purpose of money and nothing else. You must use the money in this jar sparingly to pay for investments with a high ROI. It provides the money you need for life, and it should be added to consistently until you have enough to invest in something that is guaranteed to bring back more money than you had originally spent.

I could definitely see how someone could get this jar mixed up with some of the other ones, such as Education and Give (mentioned soon). Those jars are based around spending your money on things to help your learning, and other groups, people, or charities.

The things that can come from the FFA, however, cannot be spent. The FFA can provide you with experiences you never thought were possible: the results from the money you will get from the ROI of your investment(s). You cannot spend memories. You cannot spend happiness, love, or adventures. So, while you will spend your FFA money on an investment to get money back, in the end, it's the non-physical things that you will get back in abundance from this very important account that will lead to a life of excitement and serendipity.

Long-Term Savings for Spending (10%)

The Long-Term Savings for Spending Jar (or LTSS for short) is designed to save for more expensive or bigger things in life that don't constitute as a necessity. For example, the money in this jar should be spent on things such as a holiday, car, down payment or rental for a house, events such as weddings and birthdays, or anything else with a larger fund needed. You can save up money in this account as long as you need to, but when you have enough to pay for what you want, make sure you spend it soon, so you can get back onto saving for the next thing.

Of course, the amount you may need to save for something will depend on what it is. If you have a holiday to pay for, you will save up for longer than if you just want to get a new sofa. It all comes down to how much you need for the thing you're saving up for.

You can definitely have more than one LTSS jar, but make sure to divide your 10% into each one you have. If you have $100 and one LTSS jar, put $10 in. If you have five LTTS jars, however, then put $2 in each one. Just keep in mind that it will take longer to grow these multiple accounts, as you will not have as much in each.

Education (10%)

The 10% going into your Education Jar is for any fees that come with growing yourself as a person, and should only ever be spent when needed. The most common spending for this jar would be saving up to attend college, university, or any other post-secondary program one would like to attend. While these are what most people save for, schools are just one example of the many uses for the Education Jar.

Other things that include educating oneself is attending courses and workshops that delve into areas that fascinate you. These courses may include learning a new language, instrument, or skill, studies and courses on various topics, personal development, and more. This jar also includes buying books, magazines, and webinars that will teach you something new and can make your life better. Spend it on things that truly interest you and that you would like to pursue more of an understanding on. Anything you spend your Education Jar on needs to be for things that will expand your mind about the world and the life you live while on this planet.

You are (or should be) always learning. Learning doesn't end after high school; it continues until you die. There are always new things to learn about the world and yourself, as there are limitless supplies of information to learn. You should be spending much of your life devoted to learning more and more, to bring knowledge and joy into your life; *that* is where you will truly find wisdom.

Play (10%)

The Play Jar is a fun (and quite important) fund to experience. It's the *Play Jar*, so it's gotta be a good time, right? This jar makes up 10% of your income in the system. It will positively change your view on life, and can *literally* be a life-changing experience.

The Play Jar needs to be spent every 1–3 months, depending on how much you require for the activity, but ideally every month. This jar is very important as it allows you to see a glimpse into your future life. This is done through things that your normal, everyday self wouldn't spend on. The money in this jar is to buy things that give you a view into the life you would like to have. This is the jar that you *go big or go home* with.

This jar has the money that you blow on things that you would usually say "Me? Yeah sure" about. It needs to be something that is outside of your usual, everyday shtick, so it feels like a once-in-a-lifetime opportunity (which I don't believe is a good way to live). What you spend this money on needs to be a thing or experience that allows you to feel in the moment of actually having acquired what you'd like, *when* you are abundant and wealthy, not *if*.

Some examples of spending the Play Jar would be going on a trip you never thought could happen, going to a very expensive restaurant, going skydiving, buying some fancy designer clothes, etc.

My brother wants to own a yacht, so he could save up for a few months and buy 30 minutes on the deck of the yacht he eventually wants to buy (which is the "OKTO"), because this will give him the glimpse into what his future holds. If he spends the same money on a smaller and different yacht (for a longer period, like a weekend) than the one he wants, he isn't getting the same "as if" experience of him living in the future. Do you understand?

Here is another example: Let's say you can only put aside a few bucks each month into your Play Jar. If you were to normally treat yourself to a Hershey's chocolate bar, when you have enough, you could spend it all and treat yourself to a high-end, fancy, confectionary chocolate bar instead. It's about taking what you're already doing, to the next level. Spend this money as if it is in your Necessities Jar.

Whatever you decide, it needs to be of the (as I have said already) *Go Big or Go Home* attitude. If you want that fancy house, go take a tour around it, and stand in the places you want to live in and enjoy soon. If you want a car (personally, I want a red Model 3 Tesla), go take a test drive of that car, and feel the handgrip of the wheel. The same goes for almost anything: house, car, yacht, clothing you want to wear (go buy a Gucci outfit if that's what you want to be wearing!), taking the vacation where you want to go, and so much more!

By using your Play Jar money, you get to experience what your future can and will hold. You need to be in the mindset and feeling of what you want to have and become! This is an important concept that I will discuss later in the chapter on the Law of Attraction. You will become a different person through these snapshot experiences; you will find joy in new areas of your life, and you will live in the feeling of "as if" you already have the life you desire. *That* is why this jar is so important.

Give (5%)

The Give Jar makes up the final 5% of your income. This jar is important as it presents you with the habit of giving to and helping others. The Give Jar is just 5% of your income, and you should spend it within 3 months. Of course, timing varies; you may want to save up for longer to give to a charity fundraiser, or certain times of the year when charities are looking for donations. It's all variable, so it's whatever works best for your schedule and rhythm.

The importance of the Give Jar is to create the feeling of helping another being, group, or organization. Have you ever noticed, when you help someone, you feel good about yourself? This is not the feeling of ego, but the feeling of knowing you are making an impact on another's life.

There is a significant difference between giving because you have to, versus giving because you want to. Most people donate money with a slight attitude of "Fine, take my damn money." This is not the thought you want to have when giving the money from your Give Jar. It is supposed to be given willingly and freely, with an attitude of love and joy. If you are begrudgingly giving your money to a charity, then the act of giving serves no purpose, which I'll delve deeper into, in a later chapter.

You could donate your Give money to a homeless shelter, animal charity, non-profit organization, health research, or even just a friend or person in need. Anything helps, as they say; so allow yourself to express your kindness through your Give Jar. I'll also discuss more on the reasons behind giving and receiving, in Chapter 11: Give & Receive. It has to do with reciprocity, in that when you give abundance, you receive abundance in return.

Your Give doesn't have to be huge; that is why it is only 5% of your income. Let's say you earn $1000 in a week (or $4000 a month). That's only $50 a week! Monthly would be around $200. That's about average for what people spend in a month on clothing. In comparison to the 10% ($400) for 4/6 of your monthly jars, your $200 Give spend doesn't seem like much, does it?

Now, these jars don't have to be physical; in fact, they should only be real jars if you have loose change lying around. So, while it is fun to have them physically at home, these jars are easiest to keep within your bank account. Most banks should allow you to create different accounts for different reasons to save. Make six different accounts, each with the name and percentage of how much should be added of your income. Add your money in every time you earn some. *This goes for any and all money you earn or are given.* Whether you earn weekly or monthly, each time you do, divide it into the corresponding percents for the groups.

(KEEP IN MIND: Some purchases you may have will have ongoing expenses, such as mortgages, loans, investments, etc. These are the things that screw up most people when it comes to income. So while something may seem like a one-time payment, make sure you check the metaphorical price tag to see if you will have enough in the bank to pay for the additional charges. Only spend on something with ongoing costs if you have enough to keep the payments going!)

Now that you understand the Jar System and the six areas it covers, are you ready to take control of your financial freedom? Remember to not spend your well-earned and saved money on things that serve you no purpose. It is fun to buy the occasional one-off, but don't spend wildly on things that will not get you any further financially. Don't spend more than you have available unless you can pay it off. Finally, remember *you* are the most important investment in your life. If you invest in yourself and your learning and growth, you will develop the knowledge to live the best life possible.

As my dad had once said, "Are you [all in] for your life?" Your future can only be filled with the things you love and want to do if you are financially free, so start thinking about them today.

WAYS TO MAKE MONEY

There are many different and interesting ways to make money. Nowadays, with the technology available, anyone can create the bank account they want. All you need to do is look for the opportunities that are out there. Here are some side hustles and business opportunities you can get into to create some extra cash in your life:

Start an E-Commerce Site

Starting an online business is easier than ever with the websites available now. You can use Shopify, Etsy, or any other site of the like. With these, you can drop ship or hand-ship items to your customers through your own self-made store. Shopify, for example, is very simple to set up, fairly cheap (lowest monthly rate is $29USD), and great for passive income. It is an awesome way to drop ship products easily (where the seller does not stock the items but ships them from an outside source), and can even be used to create personalized items and clothing through the apps within Shopify.

Etsy is used more for handmade items, vintage items, collectibles, and craft supplies based around specific areas. Many people go to Etsy, as they like knowing their product was made and/or owned and shipped by the creator or an enthusiast, so you know every item is crafted and handled with love.

I suggest you check out both and see what a good fit is for you. Choose what your products will be, and the audience you will be aiming your store toward. Check out some great tips that are available on YouTube videos!

Start a Blog, YouTube Channel, or Podcast

Another great idea to earn money is to start a blog website, YouTube channel, or podcast. You can start a blog about whatever you are interested in, and you can write as much as you like; a YouTube channel is a great way to get publicity and share with the world your hobbies, interests, thoughts, and more. Finally, a podcast is a great way to talk freely about whatever you want, and you can do it with friends or by yourself. Podcasts are great because you can add them to different platforms.

The way blog sites make money is from advertisements and affiliate links on the page. Your YouTube channel can get ads, sponsored brand deals, merchandise, and more. Finally, podcasts earn money from sponsors, merchandise, affiliates, and more.

Sell Items You Don't Need

Another great way to make money is by selling things in your home that you don't use anymore or need. Things that a lot of people have and don't use are old kitchen appliances, like coffee machines and kettles; books; clothes; jewelry; electronics; handmade items, and any other things you can find around your home. You can sell these things on sites such as eBay, Craigslist, Amazon, and even Facebook Marketplace, to locals in your area. Any extra cash is good cash, so have a look around and see what you can sell for a few bucks.

Flipping

Flipping is similar to the previous example, yet it is selling things that you don't own yourself. Flipping is buying items for cheap, at garage sales or thrift stores, and selling them for a higher price or their original price. This can be especially rewarding if you are able to buy something for a few bucks and sell it for $50, $100, or more! It's a great way to earn extra income, though it does take time to upload the items and their corresponding images and descriptions. If you have time, which is what a lot of people actually have, you have the possibility to earn a few extra hundred bucks every weekend. It's a hard but satisfying side hustle, and I highly recommend it.

I also encourage you to check out Gary Vaynerchuk's "Trash Talk" videos on YouTube, to see how he does it with garage sales; they are interesting, insightful, and really funny! If you take this side hustle on, imagine what you can do with all of that extra cash!

Work for Apps

Working for apps is a newer and very highly-rated way to earn some income. Apps, such as Uber, Lyft, Skip the Dishes, DoorDash, Postmates, and more, are a large source of income for many people around the world. Given, many people who work for Uber actually use it for their job, as it pays well and they are basically self-employed. However, making money with Skip the Dishes, and other food or item-based apps, is great for a good few bucks over a weekend or your spare time.

Create for Others

Websites, such as Fiverr, allow people of any and all backgrounds to earn money creating things for clients. Whether you have any prior knowledge or practice, anyone can make money online.

Many people use Fiverr and similar websites to sell their creative services, such as logo, website, and brand designing, transcribing, professional voice-overs, proofreading and editing, and more.

If you feel these aren't your strong suits, many people earn a decent amount doing silly things too. I have seen many creators on Fiverr earn $5 or more, pouring food over themselves, making odd music videos, calling you to tell you they love you, making weird gift cards, quirky Instagram captions, and so much more. Fiverr is a place for anyone to earn some quick bucks, for fun or even a steady income.

Sell Your Work

This can go hand-in-hand with creating for others, as in the last example. A great way to earn some money is to sell your original work to individuals, groups, companies, etc. Some common ideas are original artwork, music, and writing. If you are well apt with a camera, selling your photographs to stock image sites can earn you a few bucks here and there when your images are chosen.

As already mentioned, online stores, such as Etsy, are some of the best places to sell your original works, especially for artworks and hand-crafted pieces. Many artists, musicians, and writers make a good amount selling their skills on places like Fiverr as well.

Research

Do more research yourself to look into things that are more in your style and interests! Any extra cash can go a long way if used efficiently and in the right ways. Research, and decide what is best for you and your time schedule, and enjoy the benefits of working for yourself.

ooo

The next chapter is on Relationships, where you'll learn the importance of doing things for your own happiness; who you are, based on your friends; the types of people you need to hang around with, and the ones you need to drop; and finally, the importance of complimenting and being kind to others.

CHAPTER FOUR

RELATIONSHIPS

FAMILY

Family can be difficult for anyone. Sometimes they support you; sometimes they don't. When they do, it's the best feeling in the world to have those you love watching your back and cheering you on. When they don't, well, it sucks. But that is a possibility and a reality for many people. It saddens me when I hear about families not supporting other members, especially teenagers who are already trying to figure things out on their own. If families could just understand that the support of loved ones is necessary, people wouldn't be in as bad a place as they are.

If your family supports you in what you do, then great! I'm sure you're grateful for those supporting you every day, right? Don't take your loved ones for granted; they are how they are to you because you attracted those supportive characteristics. Always go above and beyond with family dynamics, and find what works best. Having a loving family is a great feeling, so enjoy it. Love them back, and stay in touch when you aren't around.

If your family does not support you, then I'm sorry. It's difficult to do the things you want when those who are supposed to be behind you are not; but don't worry—at the end of the day, it is your life. They can say and do whatever they want to diminish your goals and aspirations, but YOU are the only one who can decide what you want for *your* life, and take the steps necessary.

I believe in happiness over family; I really do. If you love your family and want to continue to see them regardless of what they think, then go for it! If family is something that is very important to you, then I don't see why you should change your views on it. What I mean about happiness over family is that, while your family will attempt to make you a different person or change how you think because they think they are wiser than you are, YOU are still in control of your life and what you do. Happiness is something that comes from life fulfillment and satisfaction, not from making your family happy. You can't let others' opinions drive your actions, especially if it is something you don't want to do.

If you are scared of talking to your family, don't be. For teens, if your parents are making you take lessons for something that you don't want to do anymore, tell them! They are just living through you, not for you. I have had many friends over the years that have had to take a certain sport, club, or course because their parents made them do it. It sucks! I always ask, "If you don't like doing it, why don't you tell them you don't want to do it anymore?" The response to this, 99 percent of the time, is, "They won't let me," or "I can't," or "They would get mad at me if I did." I'm here to tell you to face up and tell your parents you don't want to. Take responsibility for your life, and only do the things you want to do *yourself*, not what other people want you to do.

If you are an adult, stop complaining about your parents telling you that you aren't good enough, that your job could be better, that your other half isn't up to par, that you should settle down and have kids, or whatever. Take your life into your own hands. You're a grown, adult human being; you don't need your mom's approval on everything anymore—it's not a school field trip!

If you are happy, however, that is all that matters. Don't give others the time of day. Too many adults are still trying to do what their parents want from them, 40 years later. Why? Who cares about what they want? As I have already said, multiple times, it's YOUR life. Break out of your family dynamics of pressure and doubt. Figure out the things you want to do in YOUR life; say *f*** it*, and then go do them!

Stop being a puppet, and take hold of your own strings.

At the end of the day, it's your life. You choose what you do, what you want, and how you live your life, because it's yours and only yours. You shouldn't care what your family says about how you present yourself (outfits, tattoos, etc.), your goals and aspirations, who you date, what your grades are, what you earn, or what you decide to do in your future. Screw family if they don't agree. Be the person who takes a stand and asserts themselves as their *own person*. Don't be a sheep. Figure it out; say *f*** it*, and do it—you've got one life.

FRIENDS

Friends—*good friends*—are super important. I could write an entire book on the depths of friendship and social groups, but unfortunately, that is not for now. Within this part of the chapter, I will be discussing the meaning behind friends, and how these relationships impact your life *greatly*.

Who You Dine With
Which people do you associate with? Go to the movies with? Chit-chat about others with? The majority of people hang out with those they understand and relate to the most. Depending on your situation, this could be either a blessing or a curse!

When you associate and spend time with people that are in a different *vibration* or mindset, you are greatly influenced. For example, if you would say you are a generally happy person, and you hang around other happy people, you stay happy! Similarly, if you are a negative person and only hang out with other negative people, then guess what? You are going to be negative. The problem is, most people are stuck here in the negative, and find it hard to get out.

So why is it that people do this to themselves? Well, the simple answer is: they don't know! They don't understand that when they hang out with people with similar mindsets (which will be discussed in Chapter 7: Mastery), they *become* part of that mindset. They will attach it to themselves like a name tag, let it soak to their core, and even be *proud* of it. It hurts the person they truly are.

"Who you dine with is who you bond with." - James MacNeil
○○○

Who you *dine* with—meaning who you associate, hang out, and eat with—is who you *bond* with and become. If you hang out with people who are always complaining and have a negative outlook on everything, then you will *become* that type of person as well. But why do you do it?

The reason you hang out with the same type of people as you is that you are drawn to each other. For example, have you ever been a shy person? It doesn't matter what age you were or are; you have been a shy person at one point or another. So, when you've been placed into a group or hang out with others, what do you do? *Hang out with the other shy people!* How come?

You are attracted to them. When two or more people have something in common, they are drawn to each other. Have you ever heard of frequencies? We all have them; some people have lower, and some higher. People with low frequencies attract each other, and the same goes for people with high frequencies. Therefore, a positive force will *always* attract other positive forces, and negative forces will *always* attract more negative forces. Think of this as *like attracts like* (more on it, in Chapter 9: Law of Attraction). If you don't like who your friends are, start by changing yourself first. Become a positive thinker; only then will you attract more positives into your life. From here, you will begin to see how some negative friends detach themselves from you, while new positive friends develop around you.

Now you understand that *like attracts like*, and it all has to do with you and how you show yourself to the world. But why would changing yourself help? Because you need to acknowledge what has led you to associate with those people, so you can change it! When you acknowledge that you have been negative, and therefore attracting negative friends, you can start to change.

Five Friends

Who are the main five people you hang out with? That you spend most of your time with? This could be at school, work, social functions, the bar, the gym, etc. You may not believe it, but these people have a lot of influence over your life.

As I said previously, *like attracts like.* People always, without a doubt, are attracted to people with the same things as them. Whether it is income, mindset, ideologies, attitudes, habits, hobbies, or materialistic items, *all* come into effect of who you are. Usually, this is most pronounced within your closest social group. Take your five closest friends. You all hang out at the same place, doing the same things, saying the same things, and thinking the same things that you relate on the most.

If you think about it, you are exactly like those you hang around with! Let's take income, for example. If you have a job, you will (hopefully) have a rough idea of what you are earning in a year. Now, if you look at your five closest friends, they will have—without a doubt—a similar number in their bank account, usually within a $2,000 bracket. Therefore, you can only make $2,000 more than any of the friends in your group. So if you are earning $50k, and so are your friends, you are pretty much stuck at that point.

Here's another way of thinking about it: Take a cooking measuring bowl; there is a low number and a high number. The higher the number, the more volume available. If the liquid inside hits the top, then that is as high as it can go; the bowl has a max volume. The bowl's rim restricts the growth of the number, and can only hold as much as the max number allows. If not, it will overflow. This may sound good for income, but remember that the bowl's contents eventually even out to only hold as much as it can; it is held within the confines, and cannot break out. If you want to expand the limit, you need to have a bigger jug; therefore, you can grow beyond your regular *cap*, and have room to grow.

So, take another look at your income. When you are represented as the measuring bowl, you have numbers. These numbers represent your income. If you have a limit on your income, you cannot grow beyond that. You can—theoretically—break out of it, but only if you find a new max number. Therefore, you need to find new friends: more optimistic, more adventurous, and more willing to go beyond what's *allowed*, and find new ways of creating the things they desire.

COMPLIMENTS

Complimenting is one of the most important aspects of relationships. It builds trust, love, and self-esteem, and connects people in a personal way. It is a must-do for long-lasting relationships, and can totally shift weaker relationships to a point of greater connection and clarity.

When you make someone feel better—that is, with a compliment or positive acknowledgment—you heighten their self-image and happiness. There is a term called the *Impression of Increase*, coined by the author, Wallace D. Wattles, in the 1930s. The Impression of Increase is the concept that humans are always trying to be, do, learn, have, and live more to increase their satisfaction of life. Humans do this by themselves naturally, always wanting to have more, do more, learn more, etc. While you can do this for your own life, there are many ways you can have an impact on *someone else's* life, and increase *their* happiness as well. One of the main ways you impact others is by what you say. Of course, an example of this is compliments!

By complimenting others, you bring light into their life. You often feel better when you get a compliment, don't you? It's natural human behavior to feel a rush of self-esteem and confidence after receiving a compliment, and it always feels good to be acknowledged in a way that makes you feel good about yourself. It reminds you that even if you aren't particularly happy with something in your life, there are people who can see it with unbiased views and knowledge. Take an artist for example; they will see the flaws of their own work, whereas an outside view will just see the masterpiece in front of them.

Have you ever noticed the difference in how you feel if someone calls you by your name while talking to you, versus when they just talk to you as usual? At some point, definitely. It felt so much more important, didn't it? It felt like you were the center of their world at that moment. So if you can acknowledge that it feels good when it's done to you, have you ever thought about how often you do it to other people?

Next time you go to the grocery store, coffee shop, or any restaurant or public service place, take note of people's names. Most stores and companies nowadays have their staff wearing name tags. The reason nametags exist is because it creates a personal connection and allows the staff to be called by their names. As I said, most people don't do this. Why? Will it be awkward? Only if you make it awkward. Are you afraid of what they might think? It's their name! It's the prettiest thing to their ears! So don't worry about it. Try it out sometime! Say thank you to your barista, with their name. See the difference it makes in their mood; it'll change right away, because how often do they get connected on that personal level, especially while working? Not often, so start to become the person that lights someone's day up!

For close friends and family, start complimenting them more often. Comment on how they look today, that they did well on a presentation, played well in the game, cooked a nice meal, or just compliment them on being a wonderful person. Even with strangers, if you like something about them—their attitude, their humor, their outfit or hairdo, etc.—let them know! You might have seen someone before, who you admired for their outfit, presentation, etc., but never wanted to actually tell the person. What are you afraid of? A compliment is especially nice when it is from someone that has only seen you for a short amount of time or knows little about you. So take the compliment of, "I like your shirt!" and say thanks! Embrace the feeling of happiness you get.

For close friends and family, there is a compliment of sorts, called "Thank You for Being." This is when you thank someone for *who they are*, not for what they have done. It is rare for someone to thank and compliment you for being the person you are. Most of the time, a "thank you" comes from something you've done, such as grabbing the mail, doing a part of the project, putting the laundry away, etc.

The whole point of compliments is to make others feel better about themselves. If you can walk away from a conversation feeling better about not only yourself, but also about helping those around you feel better about themselves in turn, you've succeeded in the area of relationships. As you learn to compliment others, you begin to strengthen your close relationships. This forms strong bonds between you and your friends, family, partners, and everyone else! Relationships are supposed to build you up, not bring you down. Choose what kind of relationships you want, decide how they make you feel, and move toward a more optimistic, loving, and abundant social group. Using this guide for relationships will really add that spark of joy that many do not have, and it'll add years to your life!

KINDNESS

Kindness is something we all need. I'm sure I don't need to explain this one too in-depth; it is a basic fundamental of relationships, after all. I will, however, explain how kindness can be used to combat negativity, the difference between genuine and fake kindness, and why it's important to live a life of kindness.

To start, let's discuss how kindness can be used to combat negative people, yet still keep those relationships stable. Here's a great quote to explain:

ooo
"Withdraw your energy from people in your life
who are inherently energy vampires.
Practice being affectionately detached with them but always kind,
gentle, sincere and loving towards them."
- Dandapani
ooo

An *energy vampire*, as Dandapani states, is someone who drains you of life energy. These people are the ones that you feel the *life being sucked out of you* while with them. He says that these *vampires* are often family, close friends, coworkers, etc., and are harder to detach yourself from. Even when you do detach from them, you start to feel guilty about it.

Some types of people that are known as *energy vampires* are narcissists, drama queens, and those who have a victim mentality, just to name a few. Narcissists care only about themselves and their problems, and have no time for others. They are so caught up in their own lives that they don't care strongly for other people. Drama queens, though a gender-neutral term in my book, are people who like to bring others on a roller coaster of emotions (usually negative), share all of the current gossip, and are dramatic in unnecessary situations. A person with a victim mindset always thinks everyone is out to get them, and that they are treated badly compared to everyone else. This person also blames their own faults on others and things that are in their *own* control. These people are the most common types of energy vampires, so be wary of each person like this that you meet, are related to, or are friends with.

I really like the idea of being *affectionately detached* when dealing with these types of people. What Dandapani means is that while you need to detach yourself from energy vampires in your life, you still need to maintain a sense of love and kindness towards them. You are the most important person in your life, and you cannot let others bring you down, so value yourself enough to not allow others to drain you. The best thing you can do for these *vampires* is to stay distant but show only love. This way, you still maintain a relationship, albeit a distant yet affectionate one. I highly recommend practicing this way of thinking, and to start to wean out those who diminish your energy. You'll be surprised how much of a change it makes to your happiness in life, after detaching yourself from these vampires in your life—affectionately, of course!

Genuine VS Fake Kindness

Genuine kindness is much more impactful to others than fake kindness. Fake kindness is doing something nice because you were told to or have to (something that you were asked to do, where you'd say, "I'd be happy to," when in fact, you would rather be doing something else). Genuine kindness, however, is doing something out of the goodness of your heart and because you *want* to. You are grateful to be helping others, as it feels good to help others. One of the most genuine ways of achieving happiness is by being kind and helpful to others. You make others feel good, and in turn, you feel good about yourself for helping. So show more genuine kindness from now on. Be happy to help another person. It's a wonderful roundabout!

Just Be Kind
Don't overlook the importance of regular old kindness when interacting with others. Be kind. Listen to people, give advice, hold the door open, buy coffee for someone because you want to, laugh, encourage others, and be an overall friendly, good-natured person. Showing true kindness is what makes you the most genuine. You will only attract other kind people if you invest in this attitude. People love to be around happy, positive, and kind people because it makes them feel good too—it's infectious! So I ask you to just be kind. It isn't even that hard! Be a kind person and do kind things for others. Relationships blossom when this type of kindness is presented!

ooo

In the next chapter, on Health, I'll explain the three main areas of health: body, mind, and soul. Within each area, I'll tell you the best things to generate good health so you can live a healthy lifetime.

CHAPTER FIVE

HEALTH

GOOD HEALTH

I'm sure you understand the importance of having good health. You were taught when you were younger that you need to eat well, exercise, and think positively. But why do you need to? Well, it's pretty simple: you'll be very unhealthy and, eventually, die because of it. Sucks when it's put like that, doesn't it?

Having a healthy body, mind, and soul is what will help you explore the path of your life. Without these strong components, you have no way of doing the things you love to do every day. Your body, as they say, is your temple, along with your mind and soul. You need to take care of them, treat them with respect, and cherish what you have. You need a healthy body, mind, and soul to do the things you want, think well, and feel positive.

As already stated, there are three main areas of health that you need to maintain and stimulate to live healthily. These are the body, mind, and soul. Each of these areas is needed to be grown to reach your fullest health potential. Now, I will explain how each one plays an important role in your life and future ahead of you...

HEALTHY BODY
The Secrets to a Healthy Body

Eat Well

Eating healthy is a fundamental aspect for a long and happy life. You need good nutrition to allow you to live at peak performance. If not, then you are risking your own life and the joys that can come of it. I don't think I need to fully explain in-depth the types of foods that you shouldn't eat and why, but this is just a basic overview of what you shouldn't be putting into your body. Also, I'd like to preface that I am not a nutritionist; I'm just a young guy who knows what foods serve me and which do not. In any case, let's get on with some food talk.

Here are some general foods that you should avoid to live a healthier life:

High-Sugar Foods (and Beverages)

High-sugar foods and beverages are some of the worst things you can consume. Sugar is known for causing weight gain, heart disease, and diabetes, and can potentially cause acne and increase the risk of depression and other mental illnesses. It's also in almost everything. Some examples of sugary things would be soft drinks, ice cream, candy, juice, pasta sauce, ketchup, yogurt, etc.

Gluten

Gluten can cause many intestinal problems, such as inflammation, thin lining, and autoimmunity. As well, it heightens symptoms for those with celiac disease and problems with IBS, as well as the potential for causing other autoimmune diseases. Examples of foods with gluten are bread (of any type), cereals, pasta, pastries, baked goods, sauces and dressings, beer, and more.

High Carbs

Carbs (or carbohydrates) are the starches found in most foods, including grains, dairy products, and certain fruits and vegetables. While there are good carbs and bad carbs, bad carbs should be cut from your diet. These carbs can increase the risk of heart disease and diabetes. These carbs are found in foods with refined sugar, high sodium, white flour, and in those that are high in cholesterol and saturated fats. Examples of these foods are pasta and grains, beer, cereal, fast food, pears, bananas, corn, and potatoes.

I feel like I'm writing a Foods class report

Okay, so, I'm not saying you need to fully cut these foods from your diet cold-turkey; that is, cutting these foods out of your diet abruptly. When I say that you need to cut them from your meals and snacks, I mean for the majority of the time. Trust me, I *know* these foods are good, and I eat them too! The difference is that I do it sparingly.

Recently, I have decided to become vegetarian. I have always been a meat eater, but since I have become interested in the practice of Buddhism, I have decided to stop. I love animals, and humans give animals less credit than they deserve—they are very intelligent; especially the ones that people usually eat. Meat is also dead energy: it used to have energy flowing through but no longer does. Vegetables and fruits, however, are not. I don't care whether you eat meat, are vegetarian, vegan, whatever, it's just my own personal beliefs.

My family has *Cheat Day*, usually Sunday, where we are able to eat some bread and maybe a chocolate bar—nothing too crazy. I don't, however, buy two tubs of ice cream and a giant order of McDonald's! I still maintain my sense of what is a healthy limit. This *Cheat Day* is good, as it allows me to focus on healthy eating for the whole week, and then relax a bit for a day. Try doing this yourself; it will keep you on track if you find you are having a hard time sticking to a plan. I promise it is worth it!

So yes, having the occasional treat is absolutely fine. I do not recommend, however, eating these types of foods every single day. Consistently eating the same things will lead to the same results. If you eat sugary and highly-saturated foods every day, you will gain weight (among many other problems). If you eat healthy foods every day, you will become a happier and healthier being.

Exercise

Exercise, of course, is also a much-needed component of a healthy life. Physical exercise helps you to drop weight, gain muscle, and get lean and toned. It also helps to relieve stress, combat depression and anxiety, and releases chemicals that make you feel good, including endorphins, dopamine, and serotonin.

I suggest you aim to go to the gym consistently every week; a few days is best. Allow for days of rest in between so your body can strengthen and grow. With consistency, you create a habit (hey, it's that word again!) of going to the gym and creating a better you. If you don't have a gym membership, go get one. My family goes to Planet Fitness, which I find welcoming, clean, and not too costly (plus, you can bring a guest for no extra charge!). You can also do at-home workouts if you have the equipment and/or room.

I go to the gym with my parents and my brother. Usually, we go three times a week: Monday night, Wednesday night, and Saturday night. We go at night after the dinner rush, because it's normally quieter. I find it makes me feel happier, more relaxed, and ready to go to bed.

My workout routine consists of this:
- Arrive after the dinner rush (usually past 7:00 PM – 8:00 PM), after I've had dinner
- Do cardio for 30 minutes (elliptical, treadmill, stair climbing, etc.); sometimes I like to do a swap of machines at 15 minutes
- Do weights for 1 hour (arms, legs, chest, core, back), rotating between machines for targeted groups
- Go home, relax, and go to bed

You can follow the same thing, something similar, or something else entirely. As long as you are working out and strengthening your body and releasing endorphins, you are getting somewhere. Whether you do cardio or weights first, no matter what time of day you go or which gym you go to, you are increasingly creating a better you. Trust me, you won't see results at first, but after a while, you'll begin to see a decrease in fat, a slimmer and toned figure, and if you decide to, larger muscles.

It won't be fun at first; you won't see changes, you'll hurt, and you'll feel unmotivated. I promise it gets better. I have always had a dislike for physical activity, but that was because—even though I knew it was good for me—I didn't want to put the effort in. But you see, that is the key. *You* are the only one that can get you to drop that extra weight, get toned, and get buff. You can buy pills and pay trainers all you want, but until *you* take action for yourself, you will never get the body you want.

Sleep

Sleep is super important. It is a major aspect of mental and physical health, emotions, creativity, action, and overall life quality. If you are getting enough sleep every night, you should be happier, mentally stronger, and ready for the day ahead. The thing is, I rarely see this.

I always hear peers at school saying they're tired. If I go up to them and ask them how they are, I don't get a "Good, thanks," or "I'm alright." Nope. It's very rare, actually. No, instead I always get:

"I'm tired. I got three hours of sleep."

And I'm there, thinking, *Okay, cool? What else is new with you?* Personally, I feel "I'm tired" is kind of a lame excuse. I mean, of course, if someone has a reasonable explanation for being tired, like you were at the hospital all night, or you were sick or something, then okay. But I'm asking how you are as a person today, not how bad your sleeping schedule is. No offense to my friends, but usually they are the ones that made themselves tired in the first place! I ask, "So, what time did you go to bed?" And they answer, "I don't know, three or four maybe?"

What? And you're wondering why you're tired? Hmm, something doesn't add up here. You *need* quality sleep. Without it, you're tired, which means you're cranky, irritable, stressed, forgetful, have problems with coordination, and more!

You need to create a good sleep schedule. Decide how long you should sleep for (8 hours is recommended best), and then decide what time you'll wake up and get out of bed. Also, don't use technology for at least 30 minutes (preferably an hour) before bed. Your subconscious mind works over the last information in your conscious mind before you fall asleep, so think of positive things: what you're grateful for, what you will be able to do tomorrow, do some meditation, etc. If you go to bed dreading the morning, or thinking about how much you hate something, or anything else negative, your subconscious will eat on this while you sleep, and you'll wake up in a bad mood.

So, please don't put your tomorrow on the back burner because you'd rather be watching memes on YouTube, or the news at three in the damn morning. Go to bed! You need it. Think of happy, loving, and positive thoughts, and you'll wake up in a much better mood than you did yesterday!

Smoking, Drinking, and Other Drugs

Smoking, drinking, and using other drugs can immensely decrease your quality of life. Not only will they take years off of your life, but they have many various risks and health problems associated with them.

It is known that people who smoke are more likely to drink as well, which is double the amount of health risks. Smoking is known as the top preventable cause of death in North America. Cigarettes contain high levels of carcinogens that increase your chances of cancer (mainly lung cancer), cardiovascular disease and stroke, as well as lowering overall health and life expectancy. Alcohol is a known trigger for cancer, liver and heart disease, mental illness, stroke, internal bleeding and organ problems, among many other health risks. Taking drugs, such as Cocaine, Opioids, LSD, Ecstasy, Heroin, etc., will affect your psychological and physical health, can develop and/or heighten mental illness and disorders, can weaken your immune system, has a risk of potential overdose, and many other risks.

I don't understand why someone would knowingly be the reason for their eventual death, no matter how later in life it may be. Personally—and I'd hope the same goes for most people—I would not intentionally take years off of my life. I want to live a long, healthy, and happy life. By smoking, drinking excess amounts of alcohol, or using drugs, this will not happen. My life is precious—every life is—and I would not want to cut it short by taking a quick puff, sniff, or nip o' the bottle. I have never smoked, and I will never smoke. I used to have the occasional glass of wine at dinner with my parents but I don't anymore. I will not take any type of drug, liquid or otherwise, as it will disconnect me from my mind and reduce my clarity. Be smart. You have the capability to do so much self-inflicted damage with these addictions and drugs. Decide how important your bodily health is to you. Hint: it's very important!

HEALTHY MIND
The Secrets to a Healthy Mind

When I say *mind*, I don't mean your brain. Your brain is different from your mind. Your brain is merely the organ that your mind connects to and communicates from. It's the squishy, pink, physical part of your thoughts. Your mind, however, is the spiritual aspect—where your thoughts, feelings, emotions, and imagination are found. The mind cannot be contained within the brain, as it has no physical place to reside.

This part of the Health chapter is about the secrets of having a healthy mind. A healthy mind is powerful, stress free, abundant, grateful, and full of love. More will be discussed on the mind, in a later chapter, but these are a few things you can start to acknowledge, move toward, and do today.

Positivity

Having a positive mindset is one of the most important things to have, if not *the* most important. Not only that, but you also need to become the type of person that is positive. There is a difference between thinking positive and actually practicing being a positive person. Thought leads to action, but you need to know how to use these thoughts to become the most positive and loving person you know.

Being positive is something I hear so much in the world, but people brush it off as if it's nothing. It's not! It is one of the *most important* things that you achieve in life. It isn't the car, the house, the money, or the partner. It's your own happiness and love for life. Being positive is so immensely important, I cannot stress it enough.

Think positive thoughts, and think positive things of yourself and others. This creates a bundle of joy in your heart and mind, which others can see. If you are positive, others will become positive too. People want to become like the best person they know, so become the positive role model that people need!

I will touch on gratitude in a later chapter, but for now, I will tell you that you need to be grateful for what you already have in your life. If you are aware of the massive privileges and things you already have, more of those things will come to you. If you don't like getting up in the morning, then you aren't a fulfilled person, and you aren't happy with your life. If you get up and are immediately grateful that you were *able* to wake up and live, then there's something to be grateful for!

See the silver lining to life. Whether a situation is a positive or negative one, you can always see the silver lining to it. I used to find it so hard to see anything positive, especially if I was in a bad situation. Now, when I come across a deemed *negative situation*, I always stop and think about what I can be grateful for at that moment.

Be positive. It turns sadness into happiness, lack into abundance, and jealousy into gratitude. Life is so much more fun and fulfilling when you get to wake up in the morning, because *you woke up*. So stop complaining about unnecessary and minuscule things in your life, and see the bright side!

Books

Books are a great way to release positive chemicals and emotions in your mind. A good book relaxes you, makes you happy, can make you think, and is a great way to activate your mind. Reading things that interest you and make you think are the best ones.

My family and I only ever read self-development books now. We see books that won't teach us anything as being unuseful. I would much rather spend my time learning something about my own life and how to make it better, than learning about a fake town's ancient history. It doesn't serve me.

Of course, I don't hate fictional books; they just aren't for me. If you like them, however, then that's awesome. If it is something that you enjoy doing, and it makes you happy, then please, continue! I would recommend, however, that you give some self-improvement books a read. I know, they seem boring to begin; I thought so, too, when I was younger, and even until these last few years. But look at me now—I'm literally writing one!

They may not tickle your fancy to begin with, like the books you usually read, but I promise there are some really good ones out there. I will leave a list of books and other sources that I find really interesting and powerful, at the back of this book. There are a few there, but you can find more on the book's website, **www.LevelUpSteps.com**. Feel free to read them and learn from them; much of what is in this book is discussed within those books and sources as well.

People

People play a large part in your mind's health. As I've already discussed in the previous chapter, relationships impact your life in many ways. Positive or negative, these people greatly impact your mind and how it functions in a healthy, or unhealthy, way.

For your mind to be healthy, you need to be around people who bring you up: the people that are positive, treat you well, guide you, listen to you, and push you to achieve your goals. These are the ones that you want to hang around. They are in a higher vibration, and by being around them, you soak up some of their wisdom and insights into creating your own happier life.

On the other hand, if you are around negative people, your mind gets sick. These people are the ones who complain about everything, are victims, blame others, talk shit about others, and do not attempt to change or grow themselves. These are the ones that are in lower vibration and have very few goals (if any). You do not want to hang around with these people for long; avoiding them is best. Of course, remember from the last chapter, you should stay at a distance but remain *affectionately detached*. Therefore, you are still able to retain your peace of mind.

By finding new and optimistic people to connect with, you are helping to mend your mind of its past wounds. Conversing often with these people will keep you stimulated in new discussions, and will make you rethink things and change yourself to become the person you want to be. I find it so invigorating, seeing and talking with new friends that I have made within the self-development world. They guide me and give me insights, I can ask questions without being judged, and in the end, we are all learning. There is always something new to discover, and these kinds of people are excited to see where in life it takes them. Dump old relationships, and build new, healthier ones; your mind will thank you!

Hobbies

Finding hobbies that stimulate you and grow you are the best kinds. Trying new things are also ways of opening your mind to the things around you. Figure out what things you like to do; these could be reading, playing chess, taking trips, painting, writing, or going to the movies, bar, or beach, and more.

Now that you have thought of your hobbies, think: Do they serve me in my life? If your hobbies consist of things that are bad for you, maybe you should reconsider. If you go to the bar three or more times a week, grab unhealthy snacks, talk bad about others with your friends, argue with people online, and more, you're not doing yourself any favors. These types of hobbies consist of things that can tear down your healthy mind, if you do them consistently every week.

If you do, however, have hobbies that comprise of things that grow you, then keep doing them! If you love to paint, travel, learn a new language, volunteer, exercise, read or listen to inspirational messages and books, then awesome! These are the types of hobbies that will compound over time to create a more wonderful, happier, and knowledgeable you! These are the things that can take you out of your head and distract you, yet also grow you at the same time, unlike other more mind-numbing hobbies.

Now that you have acknowledged your own hobbies, decide what you need to *Cut* from your list, what you need to *Add*, and what you need to *Maintain* doing. For example, cut out the hobby of eating chocolate at school or work; this is unhealthy if done often, so replace it with something healthy instead. Add reading 10 pages of a self-improvement book every day to your list; this repeated every day will increase your knowledge and understanding of yourself. Finally, continue to go on walks at the park to get fresh air and to reset your mind. You can choose many other things to Cut, Add, and Maintain (or C.A.M.), from your list of hobbies. Do things that raise you above your own standards.

HEALTHY SOUL
The Secrets to a Healthy Soul

Meditation

Meditation is something that everyone needs to do. It slows you down and allows you to think about your life and you as a person. It connects you to the spiritual side of yourself, and opens gateways never thought possible. It's a transcendental journey to enlightenment.

There are many different ways to meditate. This could be in the form of breathing exercises, guided or self-meditation, chakra healing, visualization, and imagination. These sorts of exercises will open your mind and your soul to a different level of learning about yourself and the life you live. The problem is, many people do not think that meditation is important. They see it as a *hippie* thing to do. Whether you believe this or not, let me explain that because of the very spiritual aspect of meditation, you will learn more about yourself in a shorter amount of time than you have in all your years in formal education.

A simple thing to start doing is listening to meditation music or guided meditations on YouTube. These are quick yet powerful introductions to the art of meditation and self-healing. Something that you can do at any time of the day—whether you have something to do or have somewhere to be—is to practice mindful breathing.

Mindful breathing is simply the awareness of the number of breaths you take every minute. It is common for people to breathe far above the healthy breath limit, which is about 15 to 25 breaths per minute. These are the average breaths taken because most people are stressed, which causes faster breathing. By slowing down your breaths and counting them, you become aware of how many breaths you are taking every minute, and you can regulate the amount that you would like it to be. Slow breathing techniques help to relax you, and reduce stress. It also lowers your heart rate and blood pressure, and has been known for aiding symptoms of IBS, depression, and anxiety, among other bodily and mental functions.

If you breathe slowly and fully, you will feel less stressed, more relaxed, and happier. Try out some meditation music to do this to, or even find a guided meditation on YouTube. This can help you if you are having trouble grasping the concept. Meditation is definitely one of the areas of health that people do not speak of much, and it needs the recognition it deserves. The ancients knew about this power a long time ago, and now you do too!

Aspirations

Having aspirations, or in other terms, ambitions, is something your soul needs. Aspirations are things that you want from life, and the person you want to grow into. When you are in the mindset to think about aspirations, you begin to understand what you need in your life that will make you happy. Knowing yourself is important, and by knowing yourself, you can discover what is necessary for *you,* for your life.

Having future aspirations is good for your soul. It connects you to yourself, and allows you to discover more about yourself, so you may become a better person and live the best life possible. Being ambitious for your life is so important, which I cannot stress enough.

Aspiration comes in many forms. You probably have the aspiration to be wealthy, as most people do. This is a good start, but you need to expand on more things for your life, and for you as a person. Some questions you need to ask yourself are: Who am I? What do I want to be? What things do I want in life? Who do I need to be to have the things I want in life? Think of some other questions that you feel resonate with you. Also, don't ask *how*. The *how* will find itself to you, so don't worry about the process. It'll come to you; you just need to believe it will. Focus on what you want, and you'll receive it.

Here are the Five Areas of Life Aspirations:
- Things to Do (things you want to experience, see, do, etc.)
- Places to Go (places you want to travel to and see)
- Things to Learn (skills or information you'd like to learn)
- Possessions to Gain (materialistic things you want)
- Objectives to Accomplish (goals to reach; could also be the person you want to become)

Take a look at these, and write down a list of 5–10 things in each area that you want in life. Once you have done this, read it back to yourself, and make sure they feel right. Paste this list in a place where you'll see it every day: next to your bed, on the bathroom mirror, on the front door, etc. This will allow you to see it every day, and it will remind you what you want in life; therefore, helping you remain on target!

Start by thinking of all of the things you want in your life: people, animals, objects, experiences, and even thoughts. Say to yourself that you will live a life full of happiness, health, and prosperity in many areas. Decide who you want to become. From here, you can begin to take action in these areas, which will lead you to your goals. Remember, this is your life! Aspire to be the person you want to be, and the things you'd like to have or do. Only from here can your soul begin to flourish and become the amazing being it (*you*) is supposed to be.

TRACKING

Tracking your progress in all of the areas mentioned above is really important. By tracking your progress— past, present, and future—you start to see trends in your life. When you see how one thing brings you closer to your goal or takes you further off track, you can begin to shift what you do to create the outcomes you want.

As discussed in an earlier chapter, your time is valuable. Use this limited and powerful resource to your benefit. If you have the time to watch Netflix, browse social media, wallow in self-pity, and complain about others, then you have the time to take control of your life. So, take control of your health!

By tracking your health in these areas, you are able to see your starting point, how far and how much you have progressed, and where you are now. It doesn't end here because, from your past health mistakes, you can figure out what the trend will be for the future. Use the information from tracking to your benefit to decide what you need to Cut, Add, and Maintain (C.A.M.) in your life, to build a stronger, happier, healthier you!

Your life is special, and you need to preserve the time you have left of it. To do so, you need to be healthy. Of course, I cannot make you do anything in this chapter; it is all in your hands. I can present you with this information, but YOU need to take your physical, mental, and spiritual health into your own hands and decide: What do you really want to live a life full of?

ooo

In the next chapter, we discuss education from a school system standpoint versus education from a self-driven path. What are some things that you've always wanted to learn, were never taught in school, and never thought to pursue afterward? Well, I'll tell you all about that in the next chapter!

CHAPTER SIX

SELF-EDUCATION

SCHOOL SYSTEM

Have you ever wondered why you never learn things in school that are actually useful in life? You never learned survival techniques and first aid, how to do taxes, how to buy a house, start a business, manage money, be a good person, get advice on mental health, create good relationships, how to communicate, think, express feelings, and especially the power of self-knowledge and spirituality.

Have you ever wondered why schools have standardized testing? Why is every single student doing the same test at the same time, with the same rules applied? Not everyone learns the same way. There are different learning styles, paces, and understanding, but schools don't care about this. Here's a great quote that sums up this idea:

ooo
"Everybody is a Genius.
But if you judge a fish by its ability to climb a tree, it will live its whole life believing that it is stupid."
- Albert Einstein
ooo

If you know me, you'll know that I am not the biggest fan of schools and the education system. Personally (and this is all my own thoughts and feelings on it), I think the school system is bull. It doesn't teach me the things that will actually help in life: it enforces boundaries on learning, it teaches one-dimensionally, it doesn't encourage creativity, and it *definitely* does not want you to be your own leader in life.

I have noticed, over the past four years of high school, that all of the works I study in class are negative. Really, they all are! To Kill a Mockingbird, Animal Farm, Romeo & Juliet, Hamlet (and most Shakespeare works), Lord of the Flies, and all of the short stories within English class: Every story has death, murder, depressing matters, and hopelessness. Why? I think it's to dumb us down and make us think the same way. Why do we not learn and read about happy and positive things? Because they don't want us to see that good side of life, and they don't want us to think outside the normal box. The same curriculum has been taught since the beginning of the school system. Times have changed; education needs to catch up!

Also, I am not going to post-secondary. At the time of writing this, I have two months left of high school, and then I'm booking it out of there. I'm one of the only people in my social group that isn't going to college or university, because I don't see the point in it. The fact is that schools don't want this enforced. For example, every time I need to speak to guidance about my courses (ones that *actually* interest me), I always get asked if I'm "planning on going to university." I've told them many times that *"no, I'm not."* I've noticed—even my brother noticed when he was here two years ago—that they always say that I won't be able to get into university with the courses I'm taking, because they don't have the things necessary or something. I tell them, "Sure, but I'm still taking them."

(Now, if you actually are interested in a course for post-secondary [that means not being forced to do it], then awesome! I'm glad you will be getting something out of it that is actually what you want to learn! I see way too many people in my school that are going to university because they "should," or because their parents want them to. If it's *your* passion to become a doctor, then go! Do it! But don't let your parents or friends pressure you and make that decision for you.)

At school, students are put into a box, with very little chance of getting out of it. Author, Earl Nightingale, tells a story about a farmer who was walking in his field of pumpkins and found a glass jug. He decides to put one of the small pumpkins in the jug. The farmer returns a few weeks later to find the pumpkin had grown and squeezed itself to the shape of the jug, while the other pumpkins had grown to their full size.

This is a great analogy to showcase how restrictions can limit growth. This example can be used for many situations in life, but I feel it is a great one to explain how schools do this to students. If the pumpkin represents a student, and the jug represents the schooling system, you can easily see how you can be restricted to grow. If the school system keeps enforcing the same ideas onto every student, using the same applications, they are going to get the same result.

I'm a visual learner, which means I learn best when I have something visual added to a lesson. This could be a slideshow, a picture, textbook, etc., but I just need something to look at to learn. You may be this type of learner; you may also be an auditory or kinetic learner. Given, schools are trying to add more mixing of learning styles, but it's changing slowly. Personally, I find it hard to learn if my teacher is just standing up at the front. I need at least some writing on the board, or else everything goes over my head.

Honestly, I could go on and on forever about how schools are setting kids up to fail. They never teach anything actually important to your life, just work. Of course, work is an aspect of life, but it *isn't* what life is about. School is to make workers, not life lovers. I'm not passionate about school, because it doesn't want me to be passionate; it just wants to mold me into a sheep who follows orders. *F*** that*, I want to run my own life.

SELF-EDUCATION

Self-education, unlike formal education, can actually help you in life. With self-education, you won't have to learn Shakespeare or algebra, or study the books that schools have in the curriculum (unless you want to, of course). Self-education is the link between you and the life you desire.

You need to do things that are interesting to you, because that is where you get the most life connection and fulfillment. When you are learning about things that aren't important to you, you lose interest in what you do. You become unmotivated and unsatisfied.

Self-education is exactly what it says: the education of self. This means learning about yourself as a being, and about how to create a better life for yourself. When you realize what you want to do, to become, to have, to learn, and to live a life full of, you become knowledgeable about yourself. Once you know yourself, you have mastered life.

There are many methods of self-education. The three I can think of right now are videos, books and audiobooks, and courses. There are also ways of learning from others by teaching and learning something in turn, and finally, the concepts of *masterminds*. Harnessing these important resources will keep you engaged and excited about life, and discovering who you truly are!

Videos

I find some of the best content is the easiest to find on YouTube. It's free and has so many sources of information available for you to soak in. There are some amazing TED talks, covering a wide array of areas around life, but my favorite videos for learning are motivational videos.

These are the ones with the pumped up music and inspiring messages from well-known and well-loved authors and speakers around the world. The amount of videos like these is crazy, and there always seems to be another one in my recommendations. The music is uplifting, the words spoken are truly motivational, and they always put me in a good mood.

There are ones to help you end laziness, motivate you to work out, think positively, be grateful, love life, and so many others. Some of these sources are added at the back of this book. I would highly recommend you give them a listen to! There are also many videos about things that will interest you, so check out your passions on YouTube, and any other things you would like to learn about.

Books & Audiobooks

Books and audiobooks go hand in hand. Both are great ways of learning new information from the top motivational authors and speakers out there. Books and audiobooks are readily available in stores, online, and on apps. Don't forget to check out the list of resources and books/audiobooks I have added at the end of this book! I highly recommend each and every one I have; they have helped me to become the person I am today, and I feel they will help you too!

Books are the second easiest and cheapest way of learning about things that interest you. You can get non-fiction books on so many topics, so just pick what interests you! Whether you're interested in personal development, science, aviation, clay modeling, or anything else, there is a book for you. Just look it up in a bookstore, or on Amazon.

Audiobooks are another great way of getting the same information without having to spend the time to sit down and physically read it. My family likes to listen to audiobooks when driving to and from Toronto for courses (mentioned next). If it's a particularly good one, we'll pause it, discuss it for a while, and mention any insights we have. I like to listen to audiobooks on my way to school as well.

When I say books and audiobooks, I mean ones that can help benefit your life. I'm not saying you can't read fictional books, I just want you to get the most from your time spent reading/listening. If you can learn something new, or increase your knowledge and insight into yourself, it is far more impactful than reading a fictional work.

Courses

I'm always growing and expanding because of courses. For me, courses involve ones for self-improvement, such as life discovery workshops, speaking and communication workshops, dreaming, goal setting, relationship workshops, and spirituality learning and training. These ones have the most impact on me, so they can enlighten me like nothing else.

Other people who are interested in learning and becoming a better person attend these courses and workshops too. Most of these take place over the weekend; the ones that my family and I have been to in Toronto are usually Friday morning to Sunday evening. They are long days (usually 9 AM to 6 PM), but they have so much great information packed into every minute, so it doesn't matter to me.

There are also courses for things you might be interested in as a hobby or side-hustle. These could include painting and other art forms, physical activities, adventuring in nature, aerodynamics, learning e-commerce, and so much more. Search up things that interest you, and courses that correspond to your interests. You'll be surprised by what you find and who you will meet while there!

ooo

Check the Resources section at the back of this book for examples of books, videos, and courses you can read, watch, and take. They have all positively impacted my life, and I'd love for you to check them out!

TEACHING OTHERS

I find one of the best ways of learning is learning from other people. It doesn't matter where you meet them; it could be at the grocery store, on an airplane, at a personal development course, or it could even be a close friend of yours from childhood. Wherever you meet, and whoever it is, you never know what you can learn from someone else. I find that this is especially true when you rarely speak to the person or have never even met them before. You don't know what their back story is: you don't know where they were born, how they were raised, what lessons they learned when they were younger, or even who their favorite role model is and why.

○○○

"No man can get rich himself unless he enriches others."
- Earl Nightingale

○○○

I find it fascinating what I can learn from other people, especially those I rarely talk to or have never met before. Whether it be at school, work, a course, or anything else, I am always surprised when someone can bring something interesting and useful to the table.

For example, when I'm at school and discussing thinking habits and lifestyle with my friends, I'm always intrigued when one of them mentions something that is, 1) either a point that I'd like to talk about later in the discussion, or 2) a topic for a future time (usually something I would consider to be more advanced in regard to what we are discussing).

When I am teaching someone, and they have something to add, I find that (the majority of the time) it has more of an impact on me and/or the group than what I could have said to them. This shows me that not only are they learning what I'm teaching them, but they have understood it to an extent where they can create their own examples, insights, and importance of value on the topic, more than anything that I could have taught them myself.

Have you ever had that type of experience? When you are teaching someone—it doesn't matter if they are younger or older than you, are a family member, or your student—they seem to understand it super quickly and to a fair extent? If that has ever happened to you, which I'm guessing it has at some point or another, it had most likely taken you aback. You were probably surprised that your teachings had become understood to a point where your pupil could be more insightful than you at that moment. Yes, I know this doesn't sound how it would "normally go", but it happens more often than you would think!

There are some times when I'm at a course over the weekend, where one of the students has an epiphany. They have something to say to the teacher and/or to the group. I commonly find what they say has more of an impact of value on the group than what the trainer had to present. The entire group nods their heads in unison at the concept. They seem to understand it easier when spoken by another group member of the same level, especially when that person has been in the same boat as everyone else. I find it super interesting when someone at a course seems to explain what the teacher had said, not only in an easier way, but in a way that impacts the group in a whole new light.

A good teacher always congratulates their student on understanding themselves as a person, and grasping the concept of what they are learning. It builds trust, compassion, and mutual learning for both the teacher *and* student. This allows the student to become more knowledgeable on the subject when their teacher learns at the same time. For example, many times in my school experience, a scenario occurs where the teacher is presenting to the class. They may get something wrong with their information, are stuck on an idea, or need explanations from the students on the subject. One of the students corrects the teacher or adds insight to the lesson, resulting in the teacher learning as well. Even though the teacher was the one *teaching* the students, the *teacher* ended up being the one taking new information away from the lesson! This happens quite often actually, and I always enjoy seeing how the teacher reacts to this: usually with surprise and gratitude! Do you now see how the teacher can become the student? Take time to acknowledge these experiences, as it will definitely add importance to you *and* your teacher or student's life!

So, the next time you are talking to someone who you may view as someone lesser than you (such as in age, intelligence, past history, your student, etc.), don't be surprised when they are able to teach you something back. The whole point of this section on education is how, by teaching one person or a group, they actually will be the ones teaching you. Be supportive of those you teach, as they might, one day, teach you in turn.

MASTERMINDS

A *mastermind* is simply a group of people with similar mindsets, ideas, and goals, who are collectively working on and expanding their life's work, and achieving their dreams. These groups are used to build connections through the people involved, and aid each other in helpful insights into areas of one's life.

○○○

"The Master Mind principle: Two or more people actively engaged in the pursuit of a definite purpose with a positive mental attitude, constitute an unbeatable force."
- Napoleon Hill

○○○

As author, Napoleon Hill, stated in his 1937 bestseller, *Think and Grow Rich*, the Master Mind principle (most commonly known as a mastermind group) is two or more people discussing life purpose, solving problems, and forming new ideas in a positive light. Things that are usually discussed in mastermind groups are helpful propositions for mental attitude, business, family and friends, health, wealth, and more. Each person has a question, or needs help with a certain situation, and their peers will discuss and give ideas back. It's a give and receive group (discussed later, in Chapter 11: Give & Receive).

You cannot have a mastermind group with just yourself, because you need outside input to make constructive changes. You need accountability from someone else or a group of people. When you ask a question to yourself, your mind will tell you all of the reasons against something, because it's your logical brain having a say before anything else. If you have outside input, however, you can discuss in detail with others about why something would be good to do, without your mind getting in the way and scaring you off track. Having peers to guide you and keep track with you is a great way to stay on track to your goal. Have you ever attempted to drop some weight but never seemed to get very far? This is because you did it by yourself, and you lost faith and track of your work. If you had an accountability buddy though, you would be able to stay on track, as someone else would be involved in your progress.

Create your own mastermind if you feel you want to. It is a great way to get to know others better and at a more personal level. You can learn about yourself and those around you, gain new insights, and brainstorm new ideas. Get an accountability buddy to help you with your goal tracking (or group). They will keep track with you, and you will keep track with them. Your group should meet every week or every month, so it is regular. Each person's progress needs to be tracked and discussed by the group. When you reach your goal, start another. You'll be surprised with how much you will get done when you have people to account for your progress and give positive and helpful ideas for other areas of your life! It's a win-win situation!

○○○

Mindset is the next chapter. I have foreshadowed this chapter quite a bit, and I feel it is one of the most important ones to read. It has information on how to reprogram your thoughts, how to think positively, how to love yourself, and of course, the importance of taking action in your life!

CHAPTER SEVEN

MINDSET

While the mind is something vast and sometimes incomprehensible, it is a very powerful thing. Your mind, as discussed earlier in this book, is not your brain. As repeated from my Health chapter: *"Your brain is the organ that your mind connects to and communicates from. Your mind is the spiritual aspect, where your thoughts, feelings, emotions, and imagination are found. The mind cannot be contained within the brain, as it has no physical place to reside."* Welcome to the chapter on mindset!

Having the right mindset is the most important thing you can ever possess. Your mindset is determined by what you think and eventually do or not do. Your mindset controls your life. If you have a negative mindset, 24/7, your life will be uneventful, boring, full of anger, jealousy, and every other negative emotion you can think of. However, if you have a positive mindset, your life will always be full of possibilities, new experiences, love, and all of the emotions that make you feel good! It is up to YOU to decide the type of life you want to live.

You need to know that your mind is capable of some of the most life-changing things. It runs you, and you run it! In this chapter, you'll discover a few ways to harness the power of your mind, and how to shift your mindset from the negative to the positive. I'll make you think about your current mindset, and help you to ask yourself: "What kind of life do I want: one full of hate and resentment, or one of love and joy?"

○○○
"You are very powerful, provided you know how powerful you are."
- Yogi Bahaman
○○○

POSITIVE SELF-TALK

Positive self-talk is one of the most rudimentary elements of living a happy life. Thinking positive—not only about yourself but your circumstances, events, and other things in your life—is necessary to living a full, prosperous, and healthy life.

Most people think very negatively of themselves, and you may be included! You may think you're stupid, not good enough, not up to par. You think you may be ugly, fat, boring, or any other kind of self-deprecating attitude. There are many things you tell yourself about who you are, but mostly, they just aren't true!

You need to be your own cheerleader in life. You need to have trust in yourself that you *are* a great person, and that you *can* do the things you want to do! You shouldn't live your life putting yourself down all the time and thinking you "aren't this" or "can't do that." You need to view yourself in a positive light because, if *you* won't, how will others?

If you can recall, I discussed the idea of "I AM's" in the first chapter of this book. I talked about how you and many people are accustomed to using negative self-talk. Why? Well, you were probably taught at a young age to not show off or brag about your accomplishments and the good things in your life. This is a terrible way of thinking! You *need* to express yourself and show how worthy you are of these things!

○○○
"Be nice to yourself - it's hard to be happy
when someone is mean to you."
- Christine Arylo
○○○

No, positive self-talk is not "blowing your own trumpet." There is a big difference between the two. While showing off has a boastful "I'm better than you" attitude, positive self-talk is merely the sense of regarding yourself in a good light; you need to see the amazing person you are, and the great things you can offer and give back to the world. There's nothing selfish about it! Don't let old paradigms (thinking habits) ruin your self-image.

If you are worried about what other people think, screw 'em! People are going to talk shit, no matter what you do, so why focus on it? Block out the ones who bring you down, and embrace those who support you.

So CONGRATULATE yourself when you do something good, whether it be making someone smile, completing a checklist, achieving more progress on a goal, doing well on an assignment or task, or anything else! No matter how small it may seem to you, pat yourself on the back for doing something good.

I would suggest that once or twice a day (evening, night, or any other point), check up on yourself and congratulate yourself for something you have done. Start thinking about the things where you wouldn't usually say, "Good job, me!" The more often you do this exercise, you will begin to see yourself in a better light. Self-love, confidence, and congratulations are so important. So please, stop self-loathing, and start *self-loving*; you'll be surprised by the difference it will make in your life!

Affirmations

Affirmations are very similar to positive self-talk but are more of the practice of doing it. Affirmations are things you *affirm* to yourself, and can be used both in a positive or negative way. They are how and what you say to yourself every day. Affirmations are statements, much like the "I AMs" previously discussed, that hold truth or future truth for you, your personal character, and your life.

It's good to practice affirmations for yourself. Grab a small book and write down some things that you want to be able to say about yourself; 5–10 would be good to start. These things should be areas of life that you are wanting to improve on and get better for the future, such as self-esteem, management of yourself and your time, relationships, and more.

All affirmations need to start with or include the word *I*, because this is what makes it focused on you. If you have the word *you* in your affirmation, you are taking yourself out of the equation and are involving other people who *aren't you*. Affirmations are *about* you, so keep them focused on yourself!

It is important to speak in the present tense with affirmations, no matter if you are currently at that spot in your life yet. You need to *feel* the belief and the emotions that come through. If not, you are not connected by mind and body. This is necessary for you to create an emotional bond between you and your goals.

And no, affirmations aren't voodoo, possession, black magic, or whatever else you want to call it. They are a spiritual ritual that connects you to your most inner self, and allows you to *become* a different person. It's a way of self-empowerment and change.

Here are some examples you could use to start:
- I am healthy inside, outside, and all around me.
- Every day, and in every way, I am getting better and better.
- I am wealthy, and I make money doing what I love.
- I am worthy of a good life, full of happiness, love, and peace.
- I believe in myself and my ability to achieve greatness.
- I can do anything I put my mind to.
- And the list goes on!

You can use these ones to start, or you can create some of your own. Each one you say *has* to resonate with you on some level. If not, it's not meant for you at this moment, which is absolutely fine. Choose things that you feel connected to or that you will be connected to in the future.

By doing these every day, you will slowly change your mindset. Remember how, in one of my earlier chapters, I spoke about how a habit is formed after 21 days? Well, write these down, and say them to yourself every day for a month. If you feel better about yourself, continue to do so, and add more to your list as you progress on your journey—it's amazing what wonders affirmations can do for you and your overall life satisfaction!

ACTION

Action is the first step to results. Without action, you will never change your situation. It is a *must*. Without action, nothing will change, because nothing will be acted upon. Isaac Newton's First Law of Motion, paraphrased, is: An object at rest will remain at rest, and an object in motion will remain in motion, unless it is acted upon by an external force.

○ ○ ○

"No one is coming to save you. No one is coming to push you.
It's all up to YOU."
- Mel Robbins

○ ○ ○

Take yourself, for example; you are the object in this law. If you do not do anything to change yourself, you will stay where you are. If you are sad, in a bad relationship, broke, out of shape, or anything else you are unhappy about at this moment, it won't change unless YOU do something about it.

If you take action and become *in motion*, the things you want to change will happen. The thing is, the *external force* needs to be *you*. You need to push yourself to strive for the change you want to see. If your ideas and ambitions are not acted upon, there will be no forward movement, and therefore:

○ ○ ○

Your past is the blueprint for your future
unless you change your today.

○ ○ ○

You need to understand that YOU are the only person that can change your life. No one controls your life but you, because you are the one living it! Therefore, YOU need to take the actions that will lead you toward the life you desire! Of course, people can help you along your life's journey, but they can't be in *charge* of your journey. That is all on you.

"T.E.A.R. ™"

There is a linear path that many personal development gurus talk about, and here I have put it into my own words and terms. I call it T.E.A.R™, which stands for Thoughts, Emotions, Actions, Results.

Your life's Results are the cause of your Actions, which are the cause of your Emotions, which are the cause of your Thoughts. If you aren't happy with the results in any area of your life, you need to backtrack and see what has gotten you to that point.

ooo
"Life is 10% what happens to you and 90% how you react to it."
- Charles R. Swindoll
ooo

When you think of positive or negative thoughts, no matter what situation you're in, these thoughts lead to emotions and feelings. This is when you begin to experience the idea of what you're thinking about in your head; you're channeling your flight or fight response, which creates a physical change in your body! Once you have these feelings, there is a turning point of taking action on them. The majority of the time, people will not complete these actions; therefore, not leading to results. If you do carry out these actions, however, you will get the results you think about. Unfortunately, most people live this way but have gone down the negative path. This one is destructive to your mind and to your life, which will both become negative if you follow this route.

Here are some negative T.E.A.R.™ path examples for you to think about; figure out if any of these resonate with you:

You are overweight. What has gotten you to this point?

T: First, let's say you think about chocolate after a long day of work.

E: You really love chocolate, and you feel great when you eat some; it's your favorite treat!

A: You develop the habit of grabbing a chocolate bar every day after work, because you think you need to eat it as a reward.

R: Therefore, over time, you become overweight, or at least unhappy with your body.

You lost your best friend because of a fight. What happened?

T: You had a disagreement with your best friend on a topic you are passionate about.

E: Your friend thinks differently or has a different view on it, and you get angry.

A: You say something rude, mean, or insulting to their face, or possibly slap/punch them.

R: They take it personally and feel hurt, and they storm off. You are left without your best friend.

Do you see where I'm going with this? I'll do one more.

You experience bad service at a restaurant, and you are kicked out. Why?

T: You think the service is terrible in a restaurant, and you think your busy waiter is rude.

E: You get angry at your waiter for not being quick to take your order.

A: You start to complain and yell in frustration, and possibly refuse to pay.

R: You are kicked out of the restaurant because of your public disturbance.

Now, the last one is pretty extreme, but these can all happen. Through these examples, you can see how a negative thought can cause a negative result. However, if you start thinking positively, your results will match.

○○○
*"If you do what you've always done,
you'll get what you've always gotten."*
- Tony Robbins
○○○

For the three examples above, you could change the outcome if you use a different T.E.A.R.™ path. For the first one, think about why having chocolate wouldn't be a good idea, and come up with a different food substitute. This would lead to a different emotion of feeling good from eating healthily, which leads to actions of eating an apple (or whatever you choose), which would lead to a healthy body in the long term.

The result in the second example could be changed if you were to listen to your friend and understand what they mean. You could also "agree to disagree." These ways of communicating with your friend can protect your friendship; you just need to act positive around others.

The last example could be prevented if you saw how busy your waiter was and had compassion for how much he had to do. You could even say, "Thank you for working hard; I appreciate it!" which would change both your mood *and* their day!

With all situations you are in, you need to think of positive thoughts from the start. When you have a positive mind going into a situation, your outcome can always be seen from the positive side, and can even be affected by it. Have you ever noticed that when you aren't looking forward to something—let's say seeing someone you haven't seen in a while; and if it's someone you feel you need to see but aren't really excited about it—you're not going to have a good time. If, on the other hand, you go into it with a mood of positivity and excitement to see them, then your chat will go a lot better!

In the end, your thinking habits have caused a domino effect in your life, to create your current situation. No matter if you are in a negative or positive situation, remember that your mind doesn't care either way. It will follow the same path of T.E.A.R.™, for either side of the scale, so you need to be ready to control your results when they show.

And as I had said previously, YOU are the only one who can change your life and the direction it takes. No doctors, no friends, no family, and no motivational videos or books will make you change your negatives to positives: YOU need to do it yourself! You can get insight from others, of course, but at the end of the day, *you* need to take responsibility for your thoughts, feelings, actions, and of course—results!

Responsibility

Responsibility is one of those morals that you are taught about in school. It enforces kids to understand that they need to take control of their work and assignments to be well done and handed in on time. They are taught that timing and handling blame is a good thing. Taking responsibility for your tasks and time is important, but you need to start taking control of your *life*.

The problem is, most adults don't maintain this essential trait of responsibility. Many adults actually forget or un-learn this powerful characteristic because they go into their working lives looking to their superiors for guidance, help, and explanation in situations that they create or are involved in.

ooo

"The pack, at moments of confusion,
looks to the eyes of the leader to determine what to do."
- James MacNeil

ooo

Responsibility is underneath the Action umbrella, because you need to take responsibility for your actions. If you don't take responsibility for your actions, then you're not really controlling your life then, are you? You are in full control, and you need to start seeing it and be liable for where your life goes. If you want to drop some weight, for example, you will need to take harsh responsibility on yourself to achieve your goal. You can't just sit around all day and wait for the fat to fall off; you need to take action. Without action, there are no results. If you want to make a difference in your life, you need to take responsibility for both your actions and results.

Also, take ownership for your faults. If you messed something up, didn't get the work done or handed in on time, said the wrong thing, didn't show up, etc., take responsibility for it. Do not blame others; blaming is what children do. If you are late, don't make an excuse about the weather being bad. If you didn't get some work done on time, don't blame your group, or say that your paper went missing, you didn't know the date it was due, or whatever else you may usually say. Just tell them, "I didn't get it done," and leave it at that. You'll probably find that your teacher or boss will actually thank you for your honesty, rather than you failing to take ownership!

Excuses are for broke people—people with little-to-no life motivation. By making an excuse, you are telling everyone that you can't and *won't* control your own life. And I don't mean in the sense of money, but in the sense of an unhappy and uneventful life. That's the thing between broke and rich people: broke people don't take action or control of their life. Rich people DO, and when I say *rich*, I mean someone who lives a meaningful and fulfilled life, not just that they have lots of money (although they probably have!).

Responsibility is a good characteristic everyone should have, no matter who you are. Taking control of your life, and ownership for the actions taken, is important to build a strong character, and it should be solidly fixed into your life.

Procrastination

Procrastination is the art of putting something off until a later time. Most people are great at it in fact, and it's very common! Procrastination is such a destructive force on yourself, your life, and your dreams.

I know you've probably heard the saying, "Get it done and out of the way," right? Even if you have things you hate doing, if they need to be done, then don't put them off. Hopefully, there aren't things you hate, because "hate is a strong word," as they say, and you shouldn't be living a life of hate. If there *are* things you don't like to do, just do them anyway! When you get it done, it's finished, and you don't need to worry about it unless it's a recurring thing, in which case, don't focus on it right now; that's for the future.

Many people procrastinate because they feel something is not important to them. I've had my fair share of down-to-the-last-minute assignments handed in for school, for sure! And yes, I was stressing about it the whole time. So why do I, you, and so many people like us, daily, not do the things we need to complete?

○○○

"There is no such thing as 'Procrastination';
what it is, is it's not important to you."
- Eric Thomas

○○○

You don't finish things because they're not important to you, and that's it! Eric Thomas says he doesn't even believe in procrastination because if something is meaningful to you, you're going to do it! And if something isn't meaningful to you, you probably won't, or at most, you will "do it later."

Find meaning in what you do, even if you don't want to do it. I hate doing school work (as you already know), but I do need to get it done so I can graduate and get the hell outta there. So even though it's not important to me content-wise, I do find meaning in getting it done so I can graduate. Therefore, I find importance in an aspect of it, so I don't put it off to a later time.

Think of some things that you procrastinate on! This could be work you need to catch up on, bills to pay, people to see, exercise to do, or anything else! Once you take acknowledgment of something that you procrastinate on, start to realize what can come from doing it or finishing it. For example, if you have work to complete, once you're done, you can see your friends, family, watch movies, or whatever you want to do. If you are procrastinating on your health, eat healthily and go to the gym; you'll eventually have the body you want to have.

As of writing this, I am balancing school work with this book. I was procrastinating on my book when I began, because I didn't know what to do, so I had to think about why it's important to me and my future. I've also gotten better at getting my work done, not only on time, but sometimes early too! I've dedicated about 80% of my waking hours to writing this book: waking up at 5:30 AM and working until midnight every night. I'd like to pat myself on my back for that because, even though I don't feel like doing it sometimes, I know I want and *need* to get it done so I can have it ready before my graduation!

So, find meaning in things that you don't want or like to do. When you do, you'll get it done and have more time to do the things you want to do, such as being with those you love, doing what you love, and planning for your future!

FAILURE IS GOOD

People don't take risks because they are afraid of the consequences that may come. They are afraid to fail and to let themselves down, and those they love, and sometimes people they don't know as well! Taking risks is what builds character: you need to take risks to grow yourself and your comfort zone.

Failing is a natural part of life. It happens for a good reason, but we are taught at a young age to not fail: in school with tests, driving lessons, piano lessons, jobs, marriages, and more. Why? Because you will be classified as a *failure*. As I had mentioned in my education chapter, the school system sets up children to become dependent on success. Students are taught to learn, study hard, ace their tests, and get into a good university or college, so they can get a *good job.*

With success, however, there is a limit to how far you can grow yourself. If you are always at your maximum capability, it is only going to be an advantage for so long. Without failure, you cannot grow. If you fail at something, let's say a test, you may be annoyed at yourself for a while—maybe even hate yourself at that moment. Just imagine if you had aced that test; that's as much as you could learn! You know as much as what's on the test, and that's it. But if you had failed with a 40 percent, that means you have an error of 60 percent to improve. Therefore, the more you fail, the more you have to improve! Now, this may sound counterintuitive to you, and this may not make sense to your current success paradigm.

○○○

"Losers quit when they fail. Winners fail until they succeed."
- Robert Kiyosaki

○○○

When you fail, you open the doors of opportunity to learn. When you fail, you have the advantage over those who succeed. And yes, I know this may sound like a foreign concept to you; it may be hard to understand, especially if you were taught in school (like most people) that failure is a bad consequence.

Failure is a necessary part of growth: growth of body, growth of mind, growth of soul. Without failure, you have a cap of how much you can expand your knowledge. As you already know all that, you won't see the point of learning and improving, as you have already reached what you considered your *max*. Right? If you have failed at something, however, you can learn and grow in that area of your life, to improve it beyond what you feel is capable!

To be honest, when I was younger, I hated failing. Though I have never failed a test in school, I have done poorly at several, mainly math. Now, when I was younger, I used to take that failure to heart. I used to say things like, "Why am I so stupid?" and, "Why are all the other kids so smart and I'm not?" This is because I didn't see failure as an opportunity then, but rather as a blemish to my self-worth and capabilities. It was the determining factor of my self-perceived intellect, self-worth, and in turn, my success. Now that I have changed my outlook greatly, I can now see opportunities disguised as failures, where others do not. I take risks, and though I may sometimes fail, I always see the light at the end of the tunnel—the silver lining, as they say.

For you, it will be hard; and I'm not sugar coating it. It will, undoubtedly, be a huge pain in the ass to see the positives from your self-perceived negative situations. It takes a long time to change your thought process, to see failure as an opportunity, and to take these opportunities when they present themselves to you. You can decide for yourself if you will adopt this into your life, but I do promise you that if, and *when,* you do, your life will be forever changed for the better!

SECRET TO HAPPINESS

Saying that I have the *secret to happiness* within my knowledge is a large wager to bet. At the time of writing this, I am only 18, but I feel that within my few years of learning this path of self-development and discovery, I have noticed some things that I would consider nuggets of insight to living a happy life.

○○○
"Happiness is not something you postpone for the future; it is something you design for the present."
- Jim Rohn
○○○

I will present them to you, but in no way do you have to agree or do them. It's just that these few things have taught me much about my own happiness and influencing others around me to do the same. Life is meant to be enjoyed and full of happiness, so let's begin!

Having Fun
It's important to have fun in life! You can't live life being so serious all the time, because you will never have any fun. Having fun raises endorphins and brings you back to a state of wonder and curiosity. Having fun makes you happy and brings your heart and mind into connection with each other. When this happens, you become in-tune and in-resonance with your two most powerful emotional organs.

You must free your inner child if you want to be happy and joyous.

There is a big difference between the two terms of being childish and being childlike. Childish is living a life of self-centeredness and complaints. Someone who lives a childish life as an adult never asks how others are doing, never remembers anything important about others, and never has fun because they are always being so serious. Someone who lives a childlike life is someone who is free-spirited, full of wonder, and seeks opportunity and experience. People like this love to explore and learn new things, just like kids do! These are the people that are adventurous in taking risks, and have fun. They live a free life and are open to possibilities.

Many people think these two terms go hand-in-hand, but they don't. So many people (especially parents) tell others to not be so "happy-go-lucky" all of the time. When children get further into their school years, they are told to stop daydreaming and start acting like adults. This is enforced even further on into post-secondary education, and even the workplace.

Having fun and being a fun person is important because it allows you to express yourself and feel good. Others become attracted to your magnetic and happy vibe; you become healthier in your body, mind, and soul, and you can start to live a life of adventure and opportunity.

The Silver Lining

The problem is, most people complain that they aren't able to see the positives to everything because that's not a "realistic" way of looking at life. Sure, you could say that, and go on thinking that way and reinforcing your own self-made beliefs of negativity. You could, on the other hand, disregard that notion and begin to see life from the positive side—the silver lining, as I like to describe it.

Some of my close friends sometimes ask me: "How are you able to see the silver lining to everything? No matter what's going on, you always seem to be okay."

First, let me preface: I'm not always dandy, especially in specific situations. I am an emotional person by nature, and there's never anything wrong with that! In fact, I think every person—no matter what gender, age, past, or other—should show emotions, because it shows they are a human being and have compassion. The only times I show emotions of *weakness* to others is when there is the passing of a pet or someone close to me. When it comes to my *silver lining, always positive vibe* that people get from me, it's that I can always see the positive in a negative situation. Even if something is terrible, I can always find something good from the situation, or flip the coin and see what I have at this moment. Gratitude is so important in this concept, and I'll explain it further in a few chapters.

I always can appreciate the time I had spent with the person or animal that I'd lost. You may say, "How can I see the silver lining of my dog dying?" Well, no, you probably won't be happy that your dog died, and I hope most people wouldn't be! When I say, "See the silver lining," I mean, *see the good in the situation.* For a deceased pet, let's say that you had given them a good home and a happy life. You can look back and see how they provided many funny situations while they were still alive. So when I say *silver lining,* I don't mean you have to see everything as a positive, because losing a pet or someone close to you can hurt; just begin to see what good there was while they were still around, and the positives you can see looking back.

Stay Positive

As cliché as it is, just stay positive! I know people find this concept hard to understand. You may say it's not realistic to think this way, but why not give it the chance it deserves? Staying positive is one of the best things you can do for yourself because it keeps your spirits high and your worries to a minimum.

Being positive is very simple in its method, but very few people actually know how to be a positive person. It's actually very easy! Three basic rules to start off your positive journey:

- Continually have a happy attitude at all points in the day, no matter the circumstance.
- Have gratitude for what you already have, and for the things you have experienced.
- Be kind to others and show compassion.

These will either seem very easy or very hard for you. Everyone is different, but at the end of the day, you should know that having a positive mindset is one of the best things you can ever have: better than money, better than relationships, better than any materialistic items, memories, etc.

So, I beg you to take on the positive mindset. It'll be hard at the beginning. I know that from my own personal experience with it, but it will be so worth it. I promise your life will change when you see something good from every single situation, even if you deem it as a negative. People say to stay positive; so, what does that mean to you? All you need to decide now is: What kind of life do you want to live?

ooo

Chapter 8 is all about goals. Here, I'll explain the importance of having goals to achieve, some different kinds of goals to have, how to set them, and how to go about achieving them! Without goals, where are you going in life?

CHAPTER EIGHT

GOALS

IMPORTANCE OF GOALS

Goals are so important to have; without them, you have nothing to strive for in life. Goals are things you want to achieve in your lifetime; things you want to have, experience, learn, accumulate, live, and become. Once you have the habit of goal-setting, you can begin to follow the path to your greatest success.

Author, Earl Nightingale, gave a great analogy of how goals are necessary to get where you want to go. He gave the example of two ships, each of the same make. One of the ships has a captain and crew, with the destination mapped out and planned, knowing the exact distance and time it will take to get there. With this, the ship will undoubtedly make it to its destination. The other ship, however, has no captain or crew, no map, sails, or destination. If this ship does, in fact, get out of the harbor, it will only float aimlessly across the ocean, and will never reach its goal.

This is a fantastic analogy to show how you, as an individual person, need to have goals to get somewhere. If you do not have goals, you will float aimlessly through life. It's sad to say, but that is how the majority of people live!

Successful people are those who set goals. Why are they successful? Because they have somewhere to aim, and they know where they are going. Goals are simply the end results of future dreams.

Whether you have the goal to travel across the world, get buff, get married and have kids, do crazy adventures, or anything else, you need to have goals set to follow.

Successful people are successful because they plan. They know that to get where they want to go, they need to plan for the future, which means planning their goals. On the other hand, people who fail could be considered *failures*. These people do not set goals or have any idea of where they are going in life, and they believe that circumstances drive their lives, not their own will. They are the ship that is left to float aimlessly across the ocean of life. So, you know that there are only two paths in life that you can take. You can either be successful or you can be a failure. Being one or the other simply comes down to if you have goals or not.

So yes, having goals is super important. Why would you *not* want to live the life you've always dreamed about having? In the end, it all comes down to this: Would you like to be successful, or would you like to be a failure?

WHAT DO YOU WANT?

Now that you know you need goals to get somewhere in life, what do you want? What kinds of things do you want in your life to love and enjoy, experience, adventure into, and learn about? You know, to be successful, you need to have goals. So which ones do you want? Your goals must be meaningful and important to you. They must connect you to your dream-life, things that you thought you couldn't have.

What's terrible is that most people don't even *know* how to set goals! It's unbelievable how many people I have come across, both teenager and adult alike, who don't have goals! It's crazy, but why? This is because it was never, and still isn't, taught in schools or by parents. The only place that you probably heard about goals as a kid was from the question, "What do you want to do when you grow up?" asked by grandparents and family members you don't even know. The question shouldn't be, "What do you want to do?" (which refers to a job or career) but rather, "Who do you want to become?"

This slight change of *doing* versus *being* lets a child understand that it's alright if they have goals of making themselves into a better person and improving their own life. It shows that life isn't just centered on their future job, but it is about the journey they take to become their best self.

Your goals need to be based on things that will improve your life and make it better. Yes, they can be simple, such as a new car or house, but they can also be about making you into a better person, and someone who loves life! Shift your paradigm of goals being solely for work, to having life satisfaction in all areas.

What you need to do now is decide what you *do* want in your life, and the things you want to strive toward. Remember that if you have goals, you have a destination. If not, you won't know where you are going! The next section will explain how to set goals and what kinds of areas of goals you should have. Each category is important in its own right, and can have a very big impact on your life and the person you can and will become.

HOW TO SET GOALS

It's pretty easy to set goals, in fact. It doesn't take much time or effort; just your own will, ideas, and five minutes of your time! Write down some things that you would like, in specific areas of your life. There is a newer tradition my family has done for the last couple of years. On every January 1st, my parents and my brother and I have sat together and made a list of goals we want to accomplish in the year. We group things into areas that we want to grow in, and then write them on a big flipchart paper, and paste them in our rooms. This is so we can see our goals on the *big screen* (or paper in this instance), and see them on display for the whole year.

Relationships

Relationships are an important part of your life, or at least they should be! Relationship goals are based around people you know in your life, and improving upon those bonds. These relationships can be between you and your parents, your siblings, your love interests and partners, or colleagues and peers. Write down the people that you would like to grow your relationship with, how often you would like to meet, where you would like to hang out with them, and any other social events that you would like to attend to get to know others by. You could also write specific things, such as family game nights, hanging out with certain groups, places you like to get coffee, and things you would like to talk about.

My relationship goals, for 2019, include spending more close and quality time with my family, seeing friends more often for coffee and hangouts to chat, and finding more like-minded and spiritual people to be around!

Spiritual

Spiritual goals are things that you would like to do that grow your mind. These practices should be spiritual in nature, and by doing them, they will make you into a better person. These goals can also include spiritual practices, scheduling, or any other aspect of getting a head start on your spiritual and mental journey. Ideas of spiritual goals can include meditation, self-healing, journaling, and having a better mindset!

My spiritual section has items such as time frames for the morning (get up between 5:30 AM and 6 AM), meditating, practicing gratitude every day, journaling my thoughts daily, and listening to/reading inspirational and motivational texts, audiobooks, and videos.

Wealth

Wealth is a pretty obvious one, of course. Everyone wants money! Wealth goals must be of specific numbers from specific areas. You must be detailed in your descriptions of your wealth goals, as these will be your guidelines for your year's income. For example, you could write down the methods of obtaining these money goals, such as your work, investments, and the other side jobs for side hustles in your life. Write down the amount you want to have by a certain date or month. These need to be specific because when you see a number and date attached to goals, you subconsciously arrange your life to meet your criteria.

For my wealth section, I have written down things that I want money to be coming in from, such as online store ideas, investments, and side hustles, such as flipping items.

Health

As we have already discussed, health is another important goal to have. Health goals are what you want to look like, feel like, and how you want to do the things you want, within the year. Write down the things you need to do to obtain the health goals that you want to achieve. These could be things such as going to the gym (remember to be specific with how often you go), the fitness level you want to achieve, and how to do it, and things that you want to do once you have obtained your health goals. If you would like to complete a marathon, write down "do a marathon."

For my 2019 health goals, I have things such as going to the gym, swimming 3 or more times a week, gaining muscle, getting rid of excess fat, and maintaining an overall healthy diet and lifestyle.

Things

Goals that fall under the Things category are things you would like to obtain. This could be physical materialistic things, or it could even be experiences or things that make your life easier. Materialistic things are the most common included items on this list that you would like to have in your life. It could be a new car, new household appliances, a new house or apartment, a new computer or phone, etc. You could also write down experiences of things, such as getting proposed to and having kids (though I suppose they could fit into the relationship category). Maybe even a new pet you've always wanted! Either way, write down what you would like to have in the year.

For me, my Things list includes 3 tattoos (soon to be complete), writing a book (Hey, I'm almost there!), and to have my driving license, which I will be doing this summer. While there are many things I would like to have in this category, I still have many years to attain them. For example, I want a Model 3 Tesla car, which I have set as a goal to achieve within two years, so I still have time to work on that one!

Learn

Your Learn goals are areas you would like to understand more in depth, or new things you would like to study and practice. These goals can be for anything in your life, such as your hobbies, self-help, house tidying, investments, and anything else that you would like to grow your knowledge on. These are things that you may not be able to achieve in this year, such as learning a new language, but they should be things that you would like to continually learn more about over the course of the year.

My list has goals for learning about money management, business opportunities and systems, marketing platforms, courses I would like to attend, and hobbies I would like to get into, such as oil painting and scuba diving, and a few others.

Go

The Go category of your goals is important, especially if you want to travel or would like to travel more. Your Go category is simply places that you want to go and see and experience. This could include holidays and excursions, buildings and landmarks, or even just a place you've been to before that had brought you joy. Write down places that have inspired you in the past, or if you would like to visit at some point within the year.

My list mainly has places I'd like to go for vacations, such as Iceland, Maui, Alberta in Canada, Mexico, and more. Other things I would like to do at these places include going to the seaside or beach, going canal boating in England, climbing a mountain, etc.

Give

Giving is important; so important that I have dedicated an entire chapter to it, so keep an eye out for the Give & Receive chapter, later. Having goals for your Give category is more important than you might think, and it's very simple! The goals you need to have down for this area of life are things that you want to do for others. Helping others can be a powerful experience, and this category is all about making an impact on others by giving. Things you could write down for this one could include: donating time and/or money to charities, animal shelters, others who are not as fortunate as you, and much more. You could even start a fundraiser for something you are passionate about! It could even be as simple as being there for a friend if they have lost a loved one. Showing love, support, and interest can go a long way, and you never know what kind of an impact you can have on others!

As I love animals, on my list I have written down to volunteer at a local non-profit stray cat rescue, as well as helping out at a feral cat sanctuary, where many cats need love and affection, as well as the litter trays being done. Those are some of my Give goals for this year, and I plan on making a bigger start on them after my book is complete!

ooo

When I look at my wall of goals for the year, I see what I have already done, what I am currently working on, and what I have yet to complete. It's honestly very inspiring to see how much I have done and how well I have done some of the things on my list. I very highly recommend you to do this exercise. It's quick to do and is good for an entire year! Of course, you don't have to do it on January 1st, as I do (although it's a motivating way to start the year!), and you can continue to add to it throughout the twelve proceeding months. Anytime is a good time to start planning your future goals. Without them, where do you expect to go?

LONG TERM VS SHORT TERM

So, you have your goals thought of, developed, and written down. Now what? Well my friend, remember Chapter 7, section number two? If not, I'll give you a second to go check it…

Awesome! You better have done it now, and if not, well, I'm not angry, just disappointed…I'm only joking with you!

∘∘∘

"The Dream is free; the Hustle is sold separately."
- Mel Robbins

∘∘∘

Action! Action is, again, the main key point to getting where you want to go. This goes for goals as well because it all ties up nicely into a little bow and is gift-wrapped just for you! You can dream and set goals all you like, but until you actually take a step toward them, you will never get there!

Goals require action to come into fruition and happen. Without action, how will these goals become real? It's okay if you don't know the steps to get to your final result, but if you know where you're going, you'll get there. Just as the ship analogy suggests, if you have a course set to follow, even if you don't know what the seas may hold, you'll get there in the end. So decide on a goal, know where you are going, and you'll find your way.

∘∘∘

When deciding on what goals you want to have, don't forget to acknowledge if they are long-term or short-term goals. It is important to distinguish one from another, as you can see your vision clearly once you have them mapped out.

Short-term goals are goals that happen in a shorter length of time, depending on the situation. These goals should usually be able to be achieved within one month to a year. Goals that are short-term can include finishing up some overdue work, taking a vacation, dropping 10 lbs., having a coffee with an old friend, buying new furniture or appliances, etc.

Long-term goals either span across a long time, are continuous, or are something that must be saved for a later date. Goals that are long-term can include saving up for the car you want, getting in shape, living a healthy life, getting married, buying a house, having or adopting kids, traveling every year, improving relationships, increasing your knowledge and learning, and more.

Long-term goals can go hand-in-hand with *intentions*. Intentions are goals that take place over time, but should never have an end. They are ways of living and improving the life you want to live. Intentions are things you should be always striving to become better and better at throughout your lifetime. These are important as they help you work toward the best version of yourself that you want to be. When written down and said, these intentions will help you to reflect on what you want in life, and help to motivate you to achieve them. Also, don't forget the "I AMs" and the "I" in your Intentions!

Here are some examples of good intentions:
- I live a life of love, abundance, happiness, joy, and laughter.
- I have an amazingly close relationship with my parents and/or children.
- I am successful and fulfilled in what I do.
- I make enough money to live the life I desire.
- I am constantly learning and growing myself, and my knowledge about the world around me.

Write down some of your own ideas too. If you have a partner or spouse, write down that you live a life of happiness with them. If you want to travel, write down that you travel every month (or however often you'd like) to places that intrigue you. There are so many things that you could do, but it all comes down to what clicks with you, and what you truly want in life. In the end, everyone is different in their desires, so choose what attracts you, and state them so you can live them. So, what kind of life do you want to live, and what kind of person would you like to be by the time you die?

ooo

"Failure will never overtake me if my determination to succeed is strong enough."
- Og Mandino

ooo

Gratitude is the next chapter, which is personally one of my favorite chapters! Gratitude is an important aspect to have in order to live a happy life; are you ready to see where it can take you?

CHAPTER NINE

GRATITUDE

WHAT IS GRATITUDE?

So, what exactly *is* this thing called gratitude? You have probably heard about it over your lifetime, but have you ever really looked into it? Most people don't know what it is because it's not taught in schools or generally talked about. *Gratitude*, I cannot stress enough, is one of the *most* important aspects of happiness. So, without further ado, what is gratitude?

Do you know what the definition of gratitude is? Well, the dictionary states it as:

"Noun – the quality of being thankful; readiness to show appreciation for and to return kindness."

This is true, but there is also another way of looking at it. Gratitude can also describe a way of *being*. What do I mean by this?

○○○

"If you concentrate on what you have, you'll always have more. If you concentrate on what you don't have, you'll never have enough."
- Lewis Howes

○○○

I believe that is one of the best descriptions of gratitude that I know of. Some people like to also say, "Gratitude is an attitude," which is also very true. As I've already said, you most definitely have heard of gratitude before, but that doesn't mean you understood it! It's one of those things you hear all about on social media, TV, posters, inspirational images and videos, and more.

You've heard of it, but you probably don't listen to it. Why? Because you most likely don't know how to use it or insert it into your life. You may think, "This is too much work," or "I don't have time to think about things like that." Trust me, you do!

Gratitude has been found to improve happiness and mood, physical and mental health, relationships, self-esteem, staleness of life, and more. It's amazing what happens once you begin to feel the pride and gratitude at an emotional level, and allow it to seep into your everyday life!

Being grateful is so important. Showing appreciation and thanks for the things you already have in your life is one of the best ways you can create a happier and more fulfilling life. Everything that is good in your life needs to be seen from a view of gratitude.

There is a saying that goes like this: *"Don't complain. Someone, somewhere, is wishing for the life you have."* You need to be grateful for every single thing in your life, because there is someone in the world that is wishing for what you have, but you just brush it under the rug. Notice the things in your life that are important to you, and make your life what it is. Someone doesn't have that, but you do. Be grateful.

WHAT TO BE GRATEFUL FOR

You may be wondering what things you should be grateful for in your life; there are many! No matter how small or insignificant they may seem to you on the daily, these things are usually the ones that you would miss if you didn't have them. I call them *basic gratitudes*, although they are definitely *not* basic in my eyes. Some simple yet important gratitudes include your five senses, your limbs, and a healthy, breathing body. Each of these things helps you to live and experience all of the things in your life, so be grateful for them each and every day!

If you don't have all of these things (or at least not at their max health or power), be grateful for the ones you *do* have. I know it can tricky to get your head around at the beginning; why would you not want to focus on the things that you cannot help? Remember the last chapter? *What you focus on grows*, so focus on the things you have instead.

For example, if you like music, be grateful you have the ears to listen to the songs and artists you love. Be grateful for your eyes, as you can see your loved ones, your pets, vacation spots, and experiences. Be grateful you can smell the flowers, and the pavement after it rains, and the taste of your favorite foods. Be grateful you can feel the warmth of a fire or the hug of someone who loves you. Be grateful for your limbs, your organs, and your mind. They are all so simple, and there is so much out there to appreciate.

While I consider these few gratitudes to be *basic*, I simply mean that they are the most basic aspects of our bodies; the things we, for the majority of people, are born with that allow us to appreciate the feelings, the experiences, and adventures that make life so interesting and fun! By starting here with these simple few fundamental gratitudes, you'll open your eyes and see how good life really is, and how privileged and lucky you are, just to be alive!

○○○

"Take a step back and realize
how awesome it actually is."
- Gary Vaynerchuk

○○○

There is a quick exercise I like my friends and family to do if they need a gratitude boost or if they are feeling down. I tell them (and I want you to do this right now if you can!) to put two fingers on their wrist or their neck to check their pulse. You should, I hope, feel your heartbeat through your skin. If you do, guess what? You're alive! If you don't, well then, I would highly recommend that you see your doctor! Having a pulse is one thing, but feeling your heartbeat with no equipment attached to you is a blessing. There are many people in the world who need to be on life support, 24/7, or else their bodies will fail. Your body is working subconsciously, without you even having to think about it! So don't take these things for granted. For all you know, one day you may not have them anymore; so enjoy them, and be grateful for them while you do.

There are many other things to be grateful for that aren't centered on you as an individual. There is gratitude for having a place to live; even more so if you have your own room and have heating and air conditioning. If you have food on the table, no matter what kind, you are fortunate. If you have a loving and supportive family, and/or friend group, that is another thing to think about. Education, books, internet connection, a bed, electricity, running water, available health care, and so much more—think about all of the things that you have currently in your life, and feel the emotions that come forward.

If you don't have one or several things I have mentioned above, remember to always be grateful for what you *do* have. The more you focus on the *good* in your life, the *bad* will seem not as large and overbearing. Wake up and *feel* the gratitude for what you have. Don't complain about petty and small things. At the end of the day, if you are alive, you possess the most important thing that you have to be grateful for.

JOURNALING

In one of the earlier chapters, I explained the importance of journaling things throughout your life. It shows you where you have been, where you are currently, where you will be based on past results, as well as acknowledging what you need to change for the future.

Journaling is also important for gratitude. Every seemingly small thing in your life that makes you feel good about where you are and what you are experiencing, should be savored. It's an important reminder of the things you have.

It's important to notice and appreciate the things in your life every day. Whenever I notice something that I am grateful for, I stop at the moment and appreciate it. Whether it's hearing the birds singing outside, getting cuddles from my cats, spending time with my family, sitting and listening to a nice fire, getting an unexpected cup of tea, or even having the ability to write these words, I am grateful.

Another thing I like to do is, if I am thinking about something that bothers me, stresses me out, or is annoying, I quickly change my thought into one of gratitude. If I am thinking, "Ugh, I need to take a dog for a walk," I change it around to gratitude and, instead, appreciate the fact that I have legs and arms to take a dog out for a walk. I can be grateful for the nice weather and nature around me, and the happiness of the dog when he or she is outdoors. I do this all of the time, personally as well as to my family members. I am actually better at it than my parents, where if something is annoying them or they don't want to do something, I tell them that at least they have the things they need to do it. It jogs them out of their funk, and they agree with me. I also do this to my friends at school, as I believe that spreading gratitude and happiness is one of the best things I can do for others.

I also have started a new, daily *Gratitude Check,* as I call it, on my Instagram. If there is something during the day that reminds me of something I am grateful for, I will do a small post to my Story. It doesn't matter how big or small my gratitude is, I like to share it to get others to think of the things in their own lives. Search @jamison.smythe, on Instagram, to check out my posts!

So, start getting into the habit of writing down your own gratitudes. I suggest you get a small book; a nice simple one, in which you will write them down. Do the following: Choose 3–10 things that you are grateful for today, and write them underneath a column, titled TODAY. Do another 3–10 items under a column, titled NEAR FUTURE. Here, write down the things that you will be grateful for in the near future (about 3–5 years from now).

With the "Near Future" column, it is important you choose things that trigger some emotions. You need to be able to *feel* the emotions of love, appreciation, and gratitude in your life. Focus on how it makes you feel to *have it*, even if you don't currently do. Visualize the things you want in your future. I know it may be hard to understand how this will help you, but once you realize what you already have in your "Today" category, only then can you look ahead into your future, and focus, and be grateful for the things you will have, and the person you will be because of them.

ooo

Chapter 10 is on the Law of Attraction. What is it? Have you ever noticed when things you think about tend to happen? It's not a coincidence; so check out the next chapter to understand this fascinating and powerful law!

CHAPTER TEN

LAW OF ATTRACTION

WHAT IS THE *LAW OF ATTRACTION?*

The Law of Attraction is the name given to the universal law that gives you the ability to attract things into your life. What you have had, what you currently have, and what you will have, all stem from this universal and scientific law.

The Law of Attraction is, simply explained, the reason for the things in your life. This doesn't mean it is something you can blame, because YOU are the controller of it; it works *for you!* It works around the idea of *what you think about, you get.* The Universe, God, Source Energy, or whatever else you would like to call it, creates the things in your life, because you think about them.

The Law of Attraction pays no mind to your religious or spiritual beliefs, race, gender, age, occupation, mindset, or other. It is constantly present, working at all times, no matter when or where. It is timeless and ever-moving. It is the law that governs your life through your own thoughts.

ooo

"Whether you think you can or think you can't,
either way you are right."
- Henry Ford

ooo

111

This law has been known about for centuries, by cultures all around the globe. All of the great leaders in Earth's history had gotten to where they were because they understood this rule. This simple rule is: We Become What We Think About.

"We Become What We Think About"

This is a quote from Earl Nightingale, who understood the way thoughts and emotions played into his life and the ones around him. The saying, *"We become what we think about,"* explains how your thoughts become your world. What do I mean by this?

You become what you think about. If you think about being a sad person, you'll be a sad person. If you think about having a sickness, you'll get the sickness. If you think you can't find a partner, then you won't find a partner. If you attach a label to yourself, saying, "This is who I am, and this is my life," then you'll get exactly what you think and "ask" for.

Now, I'm going to tell you something that you may not like, but it is true: *Everything* that you have loved, hated, experienced, and lived in your life was attracted by nobody but *you*. As I have already said in this book, like attracts like—remember that? You bring the things into your life because that is what you focus on. If you focus on the bad, you'll get more of the bad; the same for focusing on the positive and getting more positives! That's nature's law.

So, while this law can help you to attract all of the things into your life that you desire, it can also be your downfall. If you focus on the negative things in your life—debt, heartbreak, or sickness—then you are going to experience those things.

Okay, let me say that I know people don't *want* sickness, or don't even know that they are at risk. If someone gets sick or has a cold, what are they supposed to think—that they *wanted* it? No, of course not! While specifics *can* be attracted, such as debt, things like colds can be brought on by negative mindsets and life situations. If you are in a bad situation, and then you get a cold, it's usually because of how you were looking at the situation. Your thoughts manifest into that cold, which you don't want and can't help. It sucks, but that is why so many people suffer from colds, illnesses, and other things.

For specific things: what you think about, comes about. When you put your thoughts out into the Universe, you get back exactly what you ask for. If you are thinking of debt, you'll get debt; if you look for dishonesty in people, you'll get dishonest people around you, because you're expecting to see it. You could also, on the other hand, think about what you *would* like instead.

What you focus on, you get more of. What you think about, you get. Your life reflects your thoughts, so think wisely. Do you want a good life experience or a bad one? What determines it are your *thoughts*.

What You DON'T Want

If you think of debt, loss, anger, pain, sickness, or lack, then that is what you are going to get. If you are angry, sad, depressed, or sick, most likely your life is filled with those things. This is because your life is based around what you think; therefore, you get more of what you *don't* want because you're always focusing on the bad stuff!

The truth is, everything that is in your life has happened because *you* made it happen. Now, I'm not saying, "You did this to yourself, so deal with it," because that's an inhumane way of looking at it. I am, however, stating that what you think about, happens. If you are in a lower mental state or *frequency*, you think of negative emotions, and ones that make you feel bad about yourself. These emotions include anger, jealousy, hate, guilt, doubt, fear, and so many others. These are what people call the emotions in the "downward spiral."

When you think of these things, you attract these things. This also goes for debt, relationship issues, illnesses, fears, and more. You are attracting the things you don't want into your life *because* you are thinking about them, and therefore being on the lower frequency. From a science aspect, frequencies attract to similar frequencies; therefore, if you think negatively, you will get negative results.

Have you ever gotten up *on the wrong side of the bed*, and just had everything in your day go to shit from there? You woke up late, tripped out of your bed, got toothpaste on your shirt, stood on your dog's tail, spilled your coffee, forgot your keys, and was late to work because of bad traffic? This, my friend, is the Law of Attraction at work in your everyday life. Your day seemed to get worse and worse, "another thing after another," because you were focusing on it. As you were in an emotional bond of frustration tied to your thoughts, that was exactly what you should expect to get.

Another example could be when you were in class, and your teacher was picking someone to read or present. You most likely thought, "Please, not me," and you were horrified when you were chosen, even though you *specifically* said you didn't want to be chosen. Have you ever gotten bills when you went to the mailbox? Well, you were probably *thinking* that you didn't want or need any more bills than you already have, but what did you find when you got there? *More of what you were thinking about!* The same concept goes for all things you don't like or don't want in life, from sicknesses to heartbreaks, gaining weight to going in debt, losing or breaking something, to your own mental health—it's all the Law of Attraction!

These things happen because they are what *you focus on*. You focus on NOT wanting them, which means you *get* them! As I've already said, the Law of Attraction doesn't care if you are thinking in the positive or negative; it gives you what you ask, or in this case, *think*, for. It doesn't care what you want or don't want, it just GIVES. You ask, it gives, and you receive—that's just how it works.

You must stop thinking of the things you don't want in your life; dwelling on your problems won't help you but will hurt you. I know it can be hard to understand why you shouldn't be focusing on a sickness, injury, money, or relationship problems. That's why you need to focus on the things you *do* want.

What You DO Want

Now, while a lot of bad things can come to you from thinking badly, imagine what the Law of Attraction can do for you if you work in harmony with it. You can have and achieve everything that you want in your life. The Law *always* finds a way of getting it to you; it's your own personal genie!

As I have already asked you many times in this book, "What do you want in your life?" This is the time to actually decide. Deciding what you want can be achieved if you know how the Law of Attraction can work in your favor. Do you want money? A healthy body, close and loving relationships, or a better job? Or is there something simple yet unattainable for you at this moment? Whatever it is, you can have it; you just need to work with the Law!

When you think positively (which I have already discussed quite a lot in this book), your life begins to fill with positivity; you start to become positive; you start to see the good in things, people, and situations—life just seems to get better!

Keep in mind that while the Law of Attraction will give you things you ask for, it may not always be in the way that you would recognize. Sometimes things show up in different areas of your life than you thought. Always be on the lookout for the manifestations of your thoughts, in every aspect of life; who knows where it will show up! Notice opportunity more often; you never know, one may lead to your desired outcome!

ooo

"When one door of happiness closes, another opens;
but often we look so long at the closed door that we do not see the
one which has been opened for us."
- Helen Keller

ooo

Emotions that will benefit you on this journey are ones that bring you in an *upwards spiral*. These emotions are ones such as happiness, gratitude, appreciation, care, love, freedom, and joy. These are the ones that make you feel good about your life, the things in your life, and most importantly, *you!*

When you begin to allow these emotions to flow into your mind, they will begin to flow into your life. You will become aware of the ever-present sense of happiness and joy that surrounds you on a day-to-day basis. Step back from your daily life, and notice all of the things you can love and be grateful for. To get the things you'd love to have, you must stop thinking of the things that you *don't* want, and start thinking about the things you *do* want! Really, it's that simple!

Live "As If"

Living "as if" is one of the *most* important steps of using the Law of Attraction in your favor. When you live "as if," you see, hear, feel, and experience something "as if" it is happening in the moment. Feeling is the fundamental reason for attracting things into your life, because emotions are energy: E-Motion = energy in motion!

When you live "as if," you get a sense of what your future holds. Visualization is another form of imagination that integrates more emotion and seeing the outcome, so I like to use that. Living "as if" is the difference between having something and not. Visualization is when you close your eyes and see what you desire in your life—the more specific the images, the better. When you have a clear image in your mind of the things you want, then the outcome will match the specifications! It's amazing what can actually happen when you practice this technique.

Now, don't forget that this can go either way: positive or negative. If you live "as if" you already have the symptoms of a sickness, the feeling of despair from debt, the lack of trust between relationships, or the fear of something going wrong, then it'll happen! But you can also live "as if" for the things you *do* want! If you want more money, visualize you are taking a vacation to your favorite place. If you want better health, visualize yourself doing the things you will do when you are healthy again, and the feeling of health throughout your body. If you are struggling in a relationship of any kind, visualize you getting on with them and having fun, laughing and enjoying yourselves. Just feel the overall abundance you *currently* have in your life, even if it hasn't physically manifested yet. Saying "I want this, I want that" isn't going to get it to you; you need the put the energy into feeling that it is *already happening.*

As I want a red Model 3 Tesla, I like to imagine myself driving it around my neighborhood for the first time. I close my eyes and see and *feel* the feeling of having already gotten the car, and having it right in front of me. I open the red door and sit down on the smooth white seats, and I hold the steering wheel in my hands. I visualize pressing on the pedal and moving, with the sound system blaring some awesome songs. I *feel* what I want to have for the future, in the moment, and can expect that is what my future will hold.

Using visualization and your imagination is an important part of your spiritual connection. You were probably taught not to daydream in school because it "distracts you from your work." What if you were thinking about your future goals? Even if you were a child, you were already on the path of attracting good things into your life, but it was taken from you. Most adults don't know how to have *imagination,* and many don't want to *because* they think it's for kids. You were given it for a reason: to imagine your future and feel the joy of things you are attracting in the moment "as if" you already have them!

○○○
"Imagination is everything.
It is the preview of life's coming attractions."
- Albert Einstein
○○○

I used to believe that nothing happened for a reason. When I was young, I thought I knew it all when I told my friends, "Yeah, nothing happens for a reason. Why would it?" And I thought I was the smartest. I used to believe in fate, but now I know better. Everything that happens in your life is for a reason, both the good and bad. The truth is: *everything* happens for a reason because YOU attract it to yourself. You bring the things into your life because you think about them and focus on them.

The same goes for *coincidence;* there are no such things as coincidence, because everything happens for a reason. If you are thinking about someone, and then they message or call you, you'll probably think "that's a funny coincidence!" No, it's not, because you attracted that into your life. A cool example was my brother. He was getting the bus home from work, and he was thinking that it would be cool if a Tesla (he wants one too) drove past and picked him up. Well, he stood there for a few minutes, and before the bus came, sure enough, a black Tesla car drove past. *What?* And even *more* funny was that it was one of our friends driving! My brother got home and told us what had happened, and we were all shocked. We knew, though, that he had attracted that to him, because he made that connection; what he thought about came about. He still had to get the bus home though, much to his dismay!

It's the people, the health, the money, the place you live, the job, and the happiness you have that result from your thoughts. The Law of Attraction doesn't care what side you fall on of good or bad, right or wrong—it just gives. It is your choice where you want to go, what you want to have, and what and *who* you want to become in your life! All it takes is a shift of thoughts and an intent to achieve them. Choose what you want in life, and focus upon that; don't dwell.

ooo

*"What you focus on grows, what you think about expands,
and what you dwell upon determines your destiny."*
- Robin S. Sharma

ooo

"THE SECRET"

There is a documentary-style film that discusses this exact concept of the Law of Attraction. It features multiple viewpoints from many well-known scientists, philosophers, authors, artists, and self-help gurus, all discussing the science and reality behind this law. The film explains both the scientific and spiritual side of the Law of Attraction, and how you can implement it into your everyday life.

There are some great examples in this film, each explaining a different scenario where the Law of Attraction plays a role in one's life. Some of these include good and bad relationships, debt and prosperity, sickness and health, visualization, self-love, and growth. It touches base on many things, not only in this chapter but throughout my entire book! I won't do it any justice by merely speaking of it, so please, for your sake, watch "The Secret."

If you enjoyed the information in this chapter specifically, I would highly recommend you watch the film. You can probably find it on Netflix or on any video streaming site or program. It is very powerful and, for me, a life-changing film. It is here that I began my journey of knowledge on the Law of Attraction, self-love, and positive thinking that I have been implementing into my life over the last few years. It helped me, and I'm sure it will open your eyes to change your own life too!

○○○
"All that we are is a result of what we have thought." - Buddha
○○○

The next chapter is on the Law of Give and Receive. This is a very important law to understand: What you give out, you receive back. While a short chapter, Chapter 11 is just as important as the previous 10, so don't skip it!

CHAPTER ELEVEN

GIVE & RECEIVE

Just like the Law of Attraction, discussed in the last chapter, another one of the universal laws is called the Law of Giving and Receiving. The law is based on the basic fundamental balance of giving to others and receiving in turn. When you *give*, you *receive*. When this equal balance flows, your life, and the lives of those around you, will begin to fill with wealth, prosperity, and abundance of positivity.

GIVING & RECEIVING

Giving is fundamental. Whether it is giving time, money, compliments, food, shelter, or affection, the main point is that you are giving. By giving, you provoke the Law of Receiving. Give and you shall receive; that is how this law works.

Giving must be done from the heart. Give freely and give willingly. The whole basis behind giving is the sense of love that comes from it. You know you are benefitting someone when you give, no matter how you do it. Have you ever noticed when you help someone, you feel good? You feel good because you know you have made another life better, and you feel good yourself because you did just that. You must give with no strings attached. The whole purpose of giving is to give and expect nothing in return; it is merely the love from within.

○○○

"You cannot build something on nothing and expect something in return."

- Raymond Holliwell

○○○

Giving must *always* come before receiving. Many people try to get away with receiving something, and say they will give later, but they never do. When you haven't established a base of the love from giving, it is against this Law to Receive.

For example, you wouldn't take a pair of sneakers from a shoe store, and say, "I'll pay for this later." Maybe, if you remember, you may go back to the store and pay for the shoes several months later. But no one does that because, 1) it's illegal, of course, and 2), it's not how the Law of Giving and Receiving works. You must give first, and only then will you receive in turn. In this example, you pay for the shoes, and then you are allowed to keep them; this shows you that you cannot receive until you give.

You need to create the base on which to build. When you build a base of giving, you can start to build a structure of receiving. Receiving is also a very important process of this law. This law is based on the two sides, giving and receiving; while opposite, they work harmoniously with one another. It is important to not only give but to receive with an equal amount of love.

THE 3 AREAS

Well-known author and speaker, Deepak Chopra, wrote a book entitled, *The Seven Spiritual Laws of Success.* The second law, which I will focus on in this chapter, is about the Law of Giving and Receiving. Chopra puts these ideas of the law into three easy to understand areas.

Here is a synopsis of The Law of Giving and Receiving:

- Bring a gift everywhere you go. The gift could be a compliment, prayer, or item. This circulates joy and wealth.
- Gratefully receive all compliments given to you. These can be spoken compliments from others, gifts of nature, or materialistic items. Be open to receiving these gifts.
- Make a commitment to keep wealth circulating in your life: wealth and prosperity of love, affection, appreciation, joy, and happiness. Wish others the love and joy they deserve.

So while you need to be ready to give, you must also be ready to receive things in your life. When you receive, you continue the flow of wealth around you and those around you. By creating the balance of giving and receiving in your life, you open the doors to new wealth. Abundance will begin to circulate around you and throughout every aspect of your life. Give with a free and willing spirit, and confidently expect the things you receive in turn.

ooo

Check out the next chapter for a few final wrap-up thoughts to finish the book!

CHAPTER TWELVE
FINAL THOUGHTS

It has been a long journey through this book, for you and for myself. You learned what I have taught you, and I have learned from writing it all out for you. It's been a journey of rediscovery for me, by relearning the things that I have understood over these last few years. This was a big feat for me to take on. I started the basic skeleton of this book when I was not even 17, and over this past year, I have discovered so much more than I thought I could. I have my parents to thank greatly for guiding me through this path over the last few life-changing years.

I'd also like to give myself a big pat on the back as well, for getting this book completed. It has taken me, as of writing this now, four and a half weeks to complete all 12 chapters and the extras within the book. I'm so proud of myself for getting this done on time, and in such a short amount. Every day, for the last few weeks, I have been up at 5:30 AM and going to bed at midnight to get this done, with very few breaks in between. My goal was to get this book finished and published for my graduation from high school this year, and I can gladly state that that goal will come to fruition within these next two months. I couldn't be happier with this book, or prouder of myself, for achieving such a big goal. A big thank you to all of you who have helped me through these last few impactful years of my life, and I look forward to more experiences in my future!

Don't forget to check out my book's website, **LevelUpSteps.com**, for more information and bonuses, and feel free to follow me on Instagram, at jamison.smythe to see where I go from here!

○○○

Within this book, I explained the 11 areas of life that you can build upon to create the best life for yourself— a life you *deserve* to have. I believe everyone should have the right to live a loving, joyous, and abundant life. Many people have the capability to, but they do not know *how* to.

I hope that through this book, you have been enlightened in one or several aspects of your life that you didn't recognize before. My goal with this book is to help you, and others like you, to see the good that life has to offer—all you have to do is take it into your own hands. You control everything in your life: your thoughts, your actions, your relationships, health, wealth, mental viewpoint on the world, and more. It is up to YOU to decide where you want to go with this. Your life is in the palm of your hand; you just need to take the steps to get there. I wish you the best of luck on your journey of self-discovery.

Infinite love and gratitude,
Jamison Smythe

RESOURCES

As mentioned throughout this book, here are some resources for you to check out yourself. The resources that I've used have changed my output on many things, and on my life as a whole. The ones I have not used yet, I will use in the future when I can; I have heard many good things about them. Check them all out, or choose ones that speak to you! I have divided them into categories of Books, Courses, and Videos.

You can find the links for these items on my website, **LevelUpSteps.com**, which will also include a larger and more in-depth list.

BOOKS

The Art of Living, Bob Proctor

"*The Art of Living* presents transcripts from legendary business speaker and mentor Bob Proctor's most popular workshop, Matrixx, and brings this wisdom to a wider audience. With this book, readers will become a student of Bob Proctor's as he teaches lessons and presents jewels of wisdom on living an extraordinary life. Among many other invaluable lessons contained herein, as a new student of Bob's, readers will learn:

- How to obtain whatever it is that's desired in life
- How to erase negative thought patterns and retrain the brain for success
- How to arrange work for maximum effectiveness..."

The Compound Effect, Darren Hardy

"No gimmicks. No hyperbole. No magic bullet. *The Compound Effect* is based on the principle that decisions shape your destiny. Little, everyday decisions will take you either to the life you desire or to disaster by default. Darren Hardy, publisher and editorial director of *SUCCESS* magazine, presents *the Compound Effect*, a distillation of the fundamental principles that have guided the most phenomenal achievement in business, relationships, and beyond."

This book really inspired me to change some of the habits I had, and how to use my time well to achieve the things I want. I really recommend this book!

Outwitting the Devil, Napoleon Hill

Outwitting the Devil was written in 1938, but due to controversial material, was hidden away from public view for over 70 years. The book details a Q&A style writing, where Hill interviews the "Devil." In this book, Hill "digs deep to identify the greatest obstacles we face in reaching our goals—including fear, procrastination, anger, and jealousy—as tools orchestrated by the Devil himself." This is not a book about religion, but a book on challenging typical thinking and living. This is the book that really changed my perspective on so many things, and I highly recommend it!

The Power of Habit, Charles Duhigg

"In *The Power of Habit*, award-winning business reporter, Charles Duhigg, takes us to the thrilling edge of scientific discoveries that explain why habits exist and how they can be changed...As Duhigg shows, by harnessing this new science, we can transform our businesses, our communities, and our lives."

The Strangest Secret, Earl Nightingale

A very short book on the *Strangest Secret,* which you will discover by reading it. It includes lessons on how to non-conform to the stereotypical societal norms, the importance of self-education and development, and more. It's a quick yet powerful and view-changing read.

Think and Grow Rich, Napoleon Hill

Think and Grow Rich details the "13 Steps to Riches" in life. In this book, best-selling author, Napoleon Hill, teaches the different areas of life that you can change to become rich; in the sense of money, health, happiness, and prosperity. Hill explains how ridding negative thoughts and focusing on goals over the long term can and will allow you to achieve the life you desire.

COURSES

10-10-10 Program, *Raymond Aaron*

Are you interested in writing your own book? Take Raymond's online course to create a book to brand you as an authority! He also offers an in-class weekend event, called the *Get Your Book Done Book Camp*, where he will guide you through the steps and answer any questions so you can get your book completed and published!

Dreambuilder® LIVE, *Mary Morrissey*

"At DreamBuilder® LIVE, Mary Morrissey will guide you through the three stages of dream building— Blueprinting, Bridging, and Building—the proven, reliable, and repeatable formula to creating a life you love living, faster and more easily than you ever imagined possible."

Millionaire Mind Intensive, *Success Resources America*

"The Millionaire Mind Intensive is a 3-day, in-person course designed to teach you proven ways to manage your money effectively, create financial opportunities for more income, and overcome the limiting thoughts, beliefs, and feelings that keep you from the wealth, abundance, and freedom you deserve and desire."

Paradigm Shift Seminar, *Bob Proctor*
"The Paradigm Shift Seminar is a 3-day course offered by Bob Proctor on how you can transform your life by changing your mental programming and thoughts. This seminar synthesizes decades of study, application, and teaching to explain what paradigms are, how they guide every move you make, how to identify your paradigms, and most importantly, how to make a Paradigm Shift."

The Speaker & Communication Workshop, *Raymond Aaron*
The Speaker & Communication Workshop is a 3-day workshop that centers around communicating effectively, influencing others, and how to become a profitable speaker and sell on stage. Here, you will learn the techniques high-earning speakers use to influence and persuade others, and how they deliver their message powerfully.

VIDEOS

Conscious Media, *Gaia*
My family has switched our monthly subscription to Netflix and changed it for Gaia. Gaia is like Netflix, but with *conscious media.* This means there are shows and documentaries about creating a better life, positive thinking, health, and ideas not usually shared with normal society. There are some really great shows and documentaries; we love to watch "Missing Links," with Gregg Braden, as well as "E-Motion," "Secret of Water," and more. I highly suggest you check it out, and learn while you watch!

I Am Affirmations, *PowerThoughts Meditation Club*
This YouTube channel has various meditation and relaxation music to listen to. My favorite videos are ones of I AM affirmations, which include voiced affirmations from the first-person perspective. I love to listen to these in the morning to set me up for a great day!

Motivational Videos, *Be Inspired*

The YouTube channel, *Be Inspired,* has many motivational videos to inspire and build you up. There are many, for different things, such as eliminating procrastination and getting work done, the importance of gratitude, morning motivation, workout motivation, paradigm shifts, and more! The videos feature audio from gurus, inspiring music, and awesome visuals. I highly recommend you check out this channel!

Trash Talk, *Gary Vaynerchuk*

Are you in need of a few quick bucks? In Trash Talk, Gary Vaynerchuk not only explains the practice of flipping items for money, but physically shows the work it takes to do it. In these videos, Gary travels to town-wide garage sales to find the best items to flip on eBay for extra cash. He explains the process, what to look for, how to search for prices, and how to recognize high-selling brands. It is not only informational but funny as well. I highly recommend watching them!

○○○

Just a final reminder to check out my website, **LevelUpSteps.com**, to find the active links for these websites, and videos and free bonuses. As well, on **LevelUpSteps.com**, there will be many more free bonuses to check out and look through, plus some full-size, full-color, print-ready documents and posters for you! There will also be a link to my personal website, **jamisonsmythe.com**, for more information about me and what I do.

ABOUT THE AUTHOR

Jamison Smythe is an 18-year-old, born and living in Ottawa, Canada. He is very close to his older brother, Scott, and his parents, Wendy and Dave Smythe. He enjoys spending time with them often, and creating lasting memories together.

Jamison is a thrill-seeker and loves to adventure and do the things in life that force him out of his comfort zone. Whether it be trying odd foods, traveling to unknown places, or taking part in something that would usually frighten most people, Jamison savors the little things in life that make it special. He relishes in the breath of life that fills him every single day, and he aims to create a life of happiness, laughter, and adventure.

Jamison looks forward to more amazing things to come in his life. He plans to travel around the world, create more life-centered content, write more books, and encourage others to think and realize their true potential. He enjoys teaching others on the amazing thing that is life!

Jamison's interest in personal development and self-growth started when his parents shared their learnings from courses they had attended and the books they had read. While not interested at first, Jamison quickly became knowledgeable on the subjects his parents discussed, and wanted to learn more. He has spent many hours with successful authors, entrepreneurs, and gurus that have taught him much about life and spirituality.

Since completing *Level Up*, Jamison is set to create his very own webinar series of the same name. Within this 12-week program, Jamison will teach you the information from the book, and explain further into the areas mentioned. Included in each weekly video will be ideas for ways you can implement these strategies into your everyday life. Keep up-to-date with his work, on his social media mentioned below!

If you would like to learn more about Jamison, visit his personal website at **jamisonsmythe.com,** or check his Instagram **@jamison.smythe,** and Twitter **@jamison_smythe,** to see where he goes next!

○○○

www.ingramcontent.com/pod-product-compliance
Lightning Source LLC
Chambersburg PA
CBHW072151090426
42740CB00012B/2228